Models of Change in Municipal Parks and Recreation:

A Book of Innovative Case Studies

Mark E. Havitz, Editor

 Venture Publishing, Inc.
1999 Cato Avenue, State College, PA 16801

Copyright © 1995

Venture Publishing, Inc.
1999 Cato Avenue
State College, PA 16801
Phone (814) 234-4561; FAX (814) 234-1651

Production Manager: Richard Yocum
Cover Designed and Illustrated by Sandra Sikorski, Sikorski Design
Primary Manuscript Editing and Maps: Michele L. Barbin
Additional Editing: Diane K. Bierly and Katherine Young

Library of Congress Catalogue Card Number 95-60987
ISBN 0-910251-77-0 ✓

Models of Change in Municipal Parks and Recreation:

A Book of Innovative Case Studies

Mark E. Havitz, Editor

Dedication

This book is dedicated to the numerous park and recreation academics and professionals who influenced me in the formative years of my career from 1977 to 1983:

Joe Fridgen, Ted Haskell, Dan Stynes, Gaylen Rassmussen, Jim Bristor, Lou Twardzik, Lew Moncrief, Don Holecek and Chuck Nelson, all from the Department of Park and Recreation Resources, Michigan State University

Carl Fenner of the Department of Parks and Recreation, Lansing, Michigan

Carl Gibson of Eaton County Parks, Grand Ledge, Michigan

Vern Hartenburg and Carolyn McClintock of the Department of Parks and Recreation, Evansville, Indiana

Steve Lampone, Jerry Darter and Jerry Day of the Department of Parks and Recreation, Kansas City, Missouri

Bill Landahl of Jackson County Parks, Blue Springs, Missouri

Jim LaPointe, Rich Schiller, Vern Hartenburg, Steve Messerli and Jack Kerr of the Department of Parks and Recreation, Ann Arbor, Michigan

Several generations of professionals are represented on this list. They work (or worked) in small towns and big cities, municipal agencies and universities. Some are close friends, others would likely no longer recognize me, nor I them, were we to meet on the street. Still others have passed on. These people inspired me even as I left Michigan in the fall of 1983 to further my academic career at Texas A&M University. Now, more than ten years later, they still do.

Mark E. Havitz
Waterloo, Ontario
August 1994

Acknowledgments

Publications are seldom the result of the inspiration or effort of a single individual, so credit for this book must be given to many people. Leon Younger of Indianapolis, Indiana, and Christine Larson of West Des Moines, Iowa, represent the best qualities of North American park and recreation professionals in the 1990s. They are creative, intelligent and highly motivated individuals, not only entrepreneurial in philosophy, but also heavily influenced by the historical human service and environmental protection ideals that have inspired our leaders for decades. The 1993 Models of Change Conference was their idea, conceived after a session at a National Park and Recreation Association Congress. Indianapolis Department of Parks and Recreation staff members deserve credit for pulling together an outstanding program on short notice, and for working behind the scenes to put on the successful 1993 conference. But, of course, most of the credit for this publication must go to the authors of the case studies and to the people who developed the programs and facilities that are described within.

Table of Contents

Section Two:
Societal and Political Change Models 69

Section Three:
Neighborhood-Based Programs............129

Introduction

This is essentially a book of case studies. The cases are described by seventeen different authors, sixteen of whom originated each individual chapter, and one who attempted to pull them together into a reasonably coherent unit. Most readers will be uncomfortable with at least some of the content and philosophies described within. Politically, the ideas come from the left and right, from both citizens and professionals. Some cases blend old ideas and new ideas, others represent ideas never before attempted. Several of the cases presented here will have a profound long-term effect on the recreation opportunities and lifestyles of residents in their communities, whereas others will have only a short-term impact. Some project outcomes will be positive, others will be negative. Some represent fundamental change in departmental policies and procedures, others are programs whose scope will affect only a small number of participants.

The challenge and mystery lies in determining which programs will work and which will not. In most cases, judgments rendered today would be premature. In the final analysis, it probably matters less which efforts will be successful or unsuccessful, but instead that the attempts were made. As such, process is emphasized over other issues such as cause and outcome. The people cited herein are working to address pressing issues facing urban parks and recreation agencies in the 1990s. These projects represent the efforts of numerous concerned professionals who believe that recreation and leisure represent positive life experiences. If there is any common theme among the programs, it is that they are designed with the hope of affecting positive change at both the individual and societal level.

One of the authors, Debra Turner of the Indiana Sports Corporation, wrote, "my philosophy of how change in government should operate is quite simple. It should be silent, cost-efficient, yet effective. A difficult philosophy that has not, as yet, been achieved." The cases described herein represent a starting point for achieving positive change.

In his management video "Passion for Excellence," Tom Peters noted that behind every successful business or innovation there is a persistent product champion, or in Peters' terms, "a monomaniac with a mission." However, it seems that recreation professionals are, by and large, a social lot. As such, most of the case studies described in this book are a result of the vision, hard work and persistence of several people. In addition to the authors themselves, the following people were the visionaries and change agents behind the stories:

Contracting Maintenance Services, Kansas City, Missouri.
Steve Lampone, Superintendent of Parks:
Jerry Darter, (former) Director of Parks and Recreation; and Mark McHenry and Mike Herron, Kansas City Parks Division.

Delegation of Authority, Arlington Heights, Illinois.
Gerald Oakes, Executive Director:
> Arlington Heights Park Board; Angelo Capulli, Superintendent of Parks; Roger Key, Superintendent of Recreation; Terry Schwartz, Superintendent of Revenue Facilities; Donna Wilson, Superintendent of Finance and Personnel; and Cathy Puchalski, Administrative Assistant.

Downtown Youth Recreation Opportunities, Des Moines, Iowa.
Don Tripp, Director of Parks and Recreation:
> Ed Hersh, Parks and Recreation Department; Connie Cook, Des Moines City Council; Lee Jensen, Metro YMCA; Wayne Ford, Urban Dreams; Steve Howell, Des Moines Police Department; and Vesta Kimble, Milton Eisenhower Foundation.

Environmental Policy, Indianapolis, Indiana.
Rob Corbett, (former) Stewardship, Grants & Property Manager:
> Chris Larson and Leon Younger, National Recreation and Parks Association; Edward Quinn, Lake Metroparks' Natural Areas Manager; and Steve Madewell, Assistant Director of Indianapolis Parks.

Indiana Sports Corporation, Indianapolis, Indiana.
Jim Titus, (former) Vice President of Operations and Executive Director of White River Park State Games:
> Mike Ford, Executive Director of White River State Games; Bill Hudnut, (former) Mayor of Indianapolis; and Jim Morris, President of Lilly Endowment.

Indy ProKids Youth Sports Initiative, Indiana Sports Corporation, Indianapolis, Indiana.
Deb Turner, Vice President of Youth Sports Initiatives and Community Relations:
> Rod St. Clair and Charles Arbuckle, Indianapolis Colts; Kathy Jordan and Malik Sealy, Indiana Pacers; Tom Weisenbach and Tony Horacek, Indianapolis Ice; Scott Doehrmann and Razor Shines, Indianapolis Indians; Randy Johnson and Shelley Hunter, Indiana Sports Corporation; Leon Younger, Indy Parks; and Stephen Goldsmith, Mayor of Indianapolis.

Intergenerational Read-To-Me Program, West Des Moines, Iowa.
Chris Larson, Assistant Director:
> Pam Gerleman, Recreation Supervisor West Des Moines Parks and Recreation; Marty Remsburg, West Des Moines Community School District Community Education; and Border's Book Store.

Lake Farmpark, Lake County, Ohio.
> Darwin Kelsey, Farmpark Administrator:
>> Jim Zampini, Al Pike and Julian Griffen, Park Commissioners; Pat O'Toole, Division Head of Special Facilities and Recreation; Leon Younger, (former) Lake Metroparks Executive Director; and Andy Baker, Sally Hosken and Rob Preseren, Farmpark department heads and programmers.

Lincoln Center Ice Arena, Columbus, Indiana.
> Geary Baxter, (former) Arena Manager, and Bill Holmes, President of Holmes Energy Services:
>> Members of the Columbus Park Board; Chuck Wilt, Director of the Parks Department; and Mike Keogh, Business Manager of the Parks Department.

The Long Center, Clearwater, Florida.
> Mark Abdo, Executive Director;
>> Fred Fisher, Philanthropist and Founder of Clearwater For Youth; Harris E. and Shirley Long, Philanthropists; Bill Carr, (former) Center Foundation Executive Director; Bob Martinez and Bob Graham (former) Governors of Florida; Ron Rabun, (former) Clearwater City Manager; John Downes, (former) Safety Harbor City Manager; William Hale, (former) Chairman of Upper Pinellas Association of Retarded Citizens; Ream Wilson, Director of Clearwater Parks and Recreation; Tom Ronald, Director of Safety Harbor Leisure Services; Herbert C. Schwartz, Center Foundation Trustee; and Hank Webb, Executive Director of Clearwater For Youth.

Neighborhood Revitalization, Anaheim, California.
> Mark Deven, Recreation/Community Services Superintendent;
>> Steve Swaim, Community Services/City Manager's Office; Mark Logan, City Attorney's Office; Bertha Chavoya, Community Development/Housing; Jeff Bowman, Fire Department; Doris Rousch, Maintenance/Streets & Sanitation; John Poole, Planning/Code Enforcement; Roger Baker, Police Department; Darrell Ament, Public Utilities; and Chris Jarvi, Parks, Recreation and Community Services.

Night Moves, Denver, Colorado.
> Theresa Rash, Operating Section Manager;
>> Wellington Webb, Mayor of Denver; George White, Denver Nuggets Community Fund; Michael Hancock, Denver Housing Authority; Michael Hancock, community youth; Youth Advisory Board Members; Oliver Van and A. B. Maxey, Glenarm Recreation Center;

Dave Rodriquez and LeMarr Miller, La Alma Recreation Center; and Dave Stalls, Deputy Manager for Recreation.

Not-for-Profit Golf Course Management, Baltimore, Maryland.
Lynnie Cook, Executive Director;
William Donald Schafer, (former) Mayor of Baltimore; Chris Delaporte, Director of Parks and Recreation (Baltimore City); Bernie Trueschler, CEO Baltimore Gas and Electric; six business leaders and executives.

Private Management of Public Golf Courses, Indianapolis, Indiana.
Leon Younger, Director of Parks and Recreation;
Mayor's Office; Service, Efficiency, and Lower Taxes for Indianapolis Commission Representatives; Indy Parks Board members; Reed Pryor, (former) Indy Parks Golf Administrator; Margaret Drew, Indy Parks Legal Counsel; Kimalie Webb, Indy Parks Strategic Marketing Manager; and Joe Kack, Indy Parks Golf Administrator.

Reinventing Recreation Programming, Waco, Texas.
Sally Gavlik, Recreation Superintendent;
Max Robertson, Bob Rhoades, Stacey Laird, J. B. Anz 'and Don Horton, Leisure Services Department; Melissa Vossmer, Assistant City Manager; Sarah Sheppard, Convention and Visitors Bureau; and Brazos Corridor Committee—City Department Committee.

Self-Reliant Neighborhood, Austin, Texas.
Robert Sopronyi, (former) Programs Division Manager;
Parks and Recreation Department staff; Library Department staff; Health and Human Services Department staff; Police Department staff; Boys and Girls Clubs staff; the Assistant City Manager; Dove Springs Advisory Board; Austin City Council; Parks Board; and Austin Independent School District staff.

The sixteen cases comprising this book are arranged into three sections. Section One consists of six cases that focus on issues related to the development and maintenance of major facilities and park lands. Section Two describes three cases developed to address specific community-wide social change and three cases based on politically-mandated change. Section Three focuses on four neighborhood-specific projects. Although the topics of emphasis vary from case to case, the general format is consistent throughout the book. Chapter authors initially framed their discussion using a ten-point outline developed by Dan McLean, Ph.D., of Indiana University. Dr. McLean's outline proved very useful for improving the consistency and interpretability of the cases. Various components of the outline have been adjusted to conform to current academic theory. For example, Section VII, Marketing to Internal and External Publics, is interpreted, whenever possible, in terms of all marketing mix components (i.e., program, price, distribution, promotion) rather than in the narrow terms (e.g., promotion, advertising) commonly used by many professionals.

Section One:
Facilities and Land Use Policies

This section includes six cases, two describing indoor/outdoor facilities in Columbus, Indiana, and Clearwater, Florida; two outlining open-space and park maintenance policies developed by Kansas City, Missouri, and Indianapolis, Indiana; and two describing golf course management policies in Indianapolis, Indiana, and Baltimore, Maryland.

One common theme in many of these cases is the attempt to successfully balance environmental concerns with business and budgetary decisions. For example, Columbus, Kansas City, and Indianapolis all found solutions that made good management and economic sense in part because they made good environmental sense as well. Another striking similarity is that the proposed solutions in each case rely heavily on input from numerous public agencies, private businesses, and nonprofit corporations. Cooperative ventures, partnerships, and facilitative philosophies dominate this group of cases. All six cases describe agency efforts to avoid go-it-alone solutions. Indicative of the cases' fresh approaches as described in this section is the solution proposed by the Long Center in Clearwater, Florida. It is so innovative that several years after the Center opened, the State of Florida is still trying to classify the venture for tax purposes appropriately.

Sociodemographic Characteristics—

Columbus

Columbus, Indiana

1990 Population:

31,802

Median Age:

34.6

Household Composition:

81.7% in families

Chapter 1

Lincoln Center Ice Arena: Self-Sufficiency Through Energy Efficiency and Total Quality Management

Columbus, Indiana

Geary Baxter
(former) Arena Manager
Lincoln Center Ice Arena

Bill Holmes
President
Holmes Energy Services

I. The Situation

In 1957 an outdoor ice rink was constructed with financial support from the Hamilton Costco Foundation (makers of infant products) and donated to the City of Columbus. This was not an unusual event in a community with a long and consistent history of public, commercial, and nonprofit sector cooperation in the provision of park and recreation services. For example, Columbus' largest manufacturer, Cummins, works with both schools and the City to allow all residents access to its extensive Ceraland Park facility which was originally constructed for exclusive use by the company's employees.

In 1974, the City replaced the original outdoor rink with an indoor arena. Unfortunately, by 1979 high utility costs were a drain on the Parks and Recreation Department's budget and threatened continuing operation of the facility. In addition, mechanical equipment and controls added in 1974 were too complex for staff members to operate effectively and attempts to get assistance in understanding and operating the system were unsuccessful. The controls could only be serviced by one local company. These problems worsened since the indoor facility's heating system adversely affected ice quality. Utility costs increased due to both these problems and the 1979 energy crisis.

The City retained a firm of consulting engineers to analyze the situation and make recommendations to reduce operating costs. Based on their recommendations, the City installed a heat recovery system which reduced utility costs by 40 percent in 1980. The heat recovery system utilized the heat created from the ice cooling compressors by recycling it into the building as a heat source.

However, by 1985 operational problems increased energy consumption above the 1979 levels and monthly utility costs rose as high as $17,500. The complex maze of old and new heating and cooling systems surpassed the capabilities of the maintenance staff. Consequently, many of the systems' components were not hooked up or operating. This problem again raised maintenance costs and rink conditions deteriorated. Excessive humidity damaged interior surfaces and water dripped on the ice. Due to high summer operating expenses and the decline in skating interest during warm weather months, the facility began to operate only six months out of the year. The number of skaters declined. This six month policy was especially problematic among serious ice skaters, who comprised the core facility users, since skating skills could not be fully developed with extended periods of inactivity. Closing the facility for the six-month period also meant that the Parks and Recreation Department had to promote every reopening extensively to re-kindle interest.

Even though actual facility operating costs were buried within the total Parks and Recreation Department budget, the fact that the arena was only 20 to 30 percent self-sufficient necessitated a large tax subsidy from the community of approximately 30,000 residents. Since a cost accounting system was not in place, operating costs hid in a variety of divisions such as special facilities and park maintenance. The annual tax subsidy approximated $250,000 to $300,000 in the early 1980s. Based on past experience and extensive study of the situation, the Parks and Recreation Department concluded that existing in-house personnel did not possess the skills necessary to operate the facility properly. As attitudes within the community and the Parks and Recreation Department grew increasingly negative, expressed sentiments toward closing what appeared to be an outdated, white elephant facility became commonplace. However, the Director of Parks and Recreation decided to look for external help to rejuvenate the facility and its programs instead.

II. Vision

The ice arena, envisioned to operate like a private business and intended to be an asset to the Parks and Recreation Department, the City, and the citizens of Columbus, became a drain on resources. The community wanted a self-sufficient and accountable arena offering an optimal skating environment all year-round.

III. Objectives

The Columbus Parks and Recreation Department developed three objectives to improve the situation and salvage the facility:

1. To set up the rink as an independent entity within the Parks and Recreation Department and to operate it as if it were a private business while maintaining availability to all citizens.

2. To hire an Arena Manager with credentials in figure skating, hockey, facility management and experience in the private sector; and, to give the Manager the authority and responsibility of achieving 100 percent self-sufficiency.

3. To hire a facility engineer in order to reduce utility and maintenance costs, improve equipment reliability, and solve the building's humidity problems. Specifically, the engineer would be charged with determining proper procedures for operating the equipment and operate all equipment accordingly.

IV. Management Paradigm Shift

The major paradigm shift involved going outside the Parks and Recreation Department to find the expertise required so the arena could function successfully as an independent entity.

V. Key Players

Key internal players included the Director of Parks and Recreation, members of the Parks' Board, the Department Business Manager, and the new Arena Manager. Facility users were the primary external advocates for change. Inefficiencies in the arena's operation, the generally poor quality of the facility and its services prompted this advocacy. Several high profile community opinion leaders were active hockey players; these individuals substantially influenced the proposed change process.

VI. Processes Undertaken to Accomplish Change

The first search, conducted in 1985, found an engineering company that would provide the required services on an ongoing basis. Holmes Energy Services, Inc. of Columbus was selected based on prior experience with the arena and its solid track record in problem solving and producing savings in operating and maintenance costs in other facilities. A five-year contract was arranged with a monthly fee to be paid by the City based on actual savings produced. Terms of the contract entitled Holmes Energy Services to 50 percent of all savings accruing from improvements in operation of equipment.

The decision to go outside the Parks and Recreation Department bruised some egos. At the Board meeting where Holmes Energy Services was hired, one employee stated that he felt that Holmes would not be able to produce significant savings because in-house personnel had already done everything possible. A Board Member responded that, because the fee was based on actual savings produced, the Parks and Recreation Department only stood to benefit from the arrangement.

In 1986 the second nationwide search sought an Arena Manager who would be employed by the Parks and Recreation Department. The successful candidate turned out to be a former professional skater with hockey and arena management experience. He had previously owned and operated a restaurant after leaving professional skating. His wife, also a former professional skater and a national champion figure skater, was hired as a teaching pro. The new management team received full authority to run all operations associated with the facility. Prior to their arrival, a Parks and Recreation Department secretary operated the main concession stand, the Park Maintenance Division was responsible for facility maintenance, and pro shop operations were contracted to a private concessionaire.

Holmes Energy initially reduced facility utility costs by installing a computerized system capable of monitoring each component of the system individually. Transition problems to the new system were minimal with the exception of objections raised by some members of the maintenance staff. During the early 1980s the facility became a de facto dumping ground for maintenance staff, many of whom were not getting along with the Park and Recreation Department's maintenance director. Maintenance staff had been regularly dispatched to the rink without being requested by the Rink Manager. The public area adjacent the rink became an employee lounge populated with extra employees who had little work to keep them busy. With permission and support from the Director of Parks and Recreation, the Arena Manager proposed cutting maintenance staff from eight to one (a staff member who really wanted to work at the rink). Under the new system, the remaining maintenance staff member reported to the Arena Manager rather than to the Park and Recreation Department's maintenance director. Two additional maintenance staff personnel were eventually added back as work demands increased.

Equipment reliability improved dramatically. The old compressors, installed in 1959, were replaced as the cost savings generated by the computer monitoring system took effect. The old cooling system was replaced with custom designed compressors, and the old air conditioning system by a heat pump. Gas usage was eliminated altogether. Overall utility costs decreased by seventeen percent. During this transition stage, Holmes Energy discovered that nearly half of the equipment purchased between the late 1950s and late 1970s had never been installed. Most of this obsolete equipment was removed from the facility.

VII. Marketing to Internal and/or External Publics

It was essential that the public be informed of the major changes that had taken place at the arena, and how those changes would benefit both the skating public and nonskating taxpayers. Initial emphasis was placed on the program component of the marketing mix; hockey and figure skating programs expanded and diversified. The hockey program began to include teams for a wider range of ages—children through adult—and a renewed emphasis on the skating club and parents groups resulted in increased activity at the arena. Rink staff reorganized all revenue producing programs, developed a competitive figure skating program, and added seven additional profit centers (see Table 1, page 8).

The advertising budget increased threefold from $400 per year. Public service announcements were also utilized and included appearances by staff members on local radio and cable television talk shows. Mass media promotion focused on human interest stories associated with ice skating rather than factual "what, when, where" information regarding the facility. For example, a whimsical newspaper advertisement featuring a man standing on two blocks of ice while being pulled by a car produced numerous inquiries regarding the rink. Although advertising increased, personal contact efforts and incentives formed the cornerstone of promotional efforts. The Arena Manager promoted skating at local schools and encouraged classes to come to the arena on field trips for free skating and instruction. On his school visits, the Manager took an educational approach by assembling second through fifth grade students for presentations during physical education classes. The Arena Manager then invited the classes to the rink for free lessons following the presentation. School groups received open invitations to come to the rink free of charge during school hours. Classes from many schools came back several times in the first year, usually in one-week instructional blocks. These efforts allowed the rink to develop skills, interest and enthusiasm among young participants during daytime hours that were not heavily programmed. Professional hockey teams and Olympic gold medal figure skaters came to Columbus to perform and hold workshops. For example, members of the National Hockey League's Buffalo Sabers sponsored and staffed high profile hockey workshops for 65 to 75 young hockey players in the past several years.

Table 1:   Lincoln Center Ice Arena Revenue Sources and Attendance by Category and Year

General Sessions	1983	1987	1993
Regular Admissions	$10,869	$9,067	$21,122
Child	N/A	N/A	9,913
Adult	N/A	N/A	4,196
Dollar Session	N/A	N/A	5,813
Group Rate	N/A	N/A	1,200
Special Sessions	N/A	1,171	N/A
Private Ice Rentals	3,181	6,334	15,579
Skate Rentals	7,700	6,825	10,560
Season Tickets	1,535	1,355	685
Non-Ice Rentals	765	2,835	N/A
Group Lessons	7,624	47	26,156
Figure Skating Club	9,007	10,441	24,225
Columbus Youth Hockey	13,245	23,814	28,953
Subtotals	**$54,928**	**$61,889**	**$127,280**
Regular Groups, Events and Concessions			
Concessions	$3,000	$10,298	$28,878
Birthday Parties	N/A	455	1,200
Stick and Puck	N/A	N/A	350
Morning Ice	1,284	8,477	14,120
Summer Figure School	N/A	14,215	23,051
Group Lessons	7,624	12,571	21,146
House League Hockey	9,852	12,787	15,762
Adult Hockey	923	2,191	3,700
Summer Hockey Camp	N/A	6,300	15,185
Summer Hockey League	N/A	6,450	10,826
Broomball	N/A	N/A	2,450
Locker Rental	N/A	N/A	1,500
Small Rink Rental	N/A	2,075	3,952
Management Expense	N/A	N/A	24,802
Pro Shop	630	18,683	65,784
Subtotals	**$23,313**	**$94,503**	**$232,706**
Combined Totals	**$78,241**	**$156,392**	**$359,986**
Public Session Attendance	**12,897**	**18,654**	**22,395**

VIII. Impact of Change on the Agency

Improvements introduced by Holmes Energy Services before 1990 lowered the average monthly utility cost by 67 percent to $3,500, saving the Parks and Recreation Department approximately $100,000 per year. In addition, the number of Parks and Recreation Department personnel working at the rink was reduced from twelve to six, and mechanical and electrical equipment maintenance costs dropped by $15,000 per year. The original refrigeration equipment, plagued by age and obsolescence, was replaced in 1990 at a cost $100,000 below the earlier estimates due to changes recommended by Holmes Energy Services. These cumulative savings resulted from Holmes' intimate involvement with the arena for five years. Following the installation of new refrigeration equipment, utility costs dropped an additional ten percent. In total, the new equipment and maintenance policies increased the arena's self-sufficiency level from 28 percent in 1985 to 84 percent in 1993. One hundred percent self-sufficiency is projected by 1995.

IX. Impact of Change on the Community

Over the past eight years, the availability, usage levels, and image of the facility improved in several ways. Operating hours expanded to 6 a.m. to 11 p.m. and the arena season extended to eleven months per year instead of six. This extended season and increased ice availability improved both the quantity and quality of Columbus residents' skating experiences. The arena also serves members of the nonskating public. For example, the Parks and Recreation Department offers the facility to local high schools for their after-prom parties during the annual May maintenance shutdown.

Public areas within the facility were cleaned up and remodeled. Building maintenance levels improved despite reduced staff levels. The maintenance staff were chosen based on their willingness to work at the rink and report in-house to arena management rather than to the centralized maintenance system. Parks and Recreation Department employees, when barred from using the lobby as a coffee lounge, were provided an off-stage area for their breaks. This policy not only improved the atmosphere of the lobby for skaters and other visitors, but also it also gave employees more privacy during their breaks.

Optimal skating conditions evolved because modernized, properly functioning equipment greatly improved ice quality. The quality of the skating improved to the point that over a dozen students from throughout the United States and South America come to the Lincoln Center annually to train with its skating pro. Competitive skaters from Columbus are doing very well; four national level competitors emerged from Columbus in recent years. Hockey teams from Columbus also performed very well in tournaments in the U.S. and Canada. Columbus teams won four consecutive Indiana State Hockey Championships, were named the Silver Stick Champions—symbolic of the top ranked hockey team—and Columbus had the highest percentage of kids drafted to Team Indiana in recent years.

X. Measurement of the Outcome

Five tangible measures of facility efficiency and effectiveness have been used to date.

First, the key element in many of the improvements was the installation of a facility monitoring system that continuously monitors rink conditions, energy consumption and equipment operation. This monitoring system also provides accurate quantitative measures of the performance of the arena's equipment.

Second, Holmes Energy Services submits detailed monthly reports on actual utility costs and savings as a part of their contract with the Parks and Recreation Department.

Third, the establishment of an internal cost accounting system identifies income and expenses of the facility separately within the overall Parks and Recreation Department financial system so that self-sufficiency levels can be determined.

Fourth, the system for determining the actual number of skaters improved and a computerized tracking system was initiated. Prior to 1985, only basic attendance figures were compiled. The Parks and Recreation Department now collects accurate data on a variety of sociodemographic and behavioral characteristics of facility users. Data on patrons' ages, season ticket usage, special events attendance, and free pass usage is available (see Table 1, page 8). In addition, the Parks and Recreation Department monitors attendance patterns of groups from schools and Big Brothers/Big Sisters who use the facility free of charge.

The final measure of effectiveness is external recognition. The arena received two awards for Parks and Recreation Departmental efforts to reduce utility costs. The arena was one of 51 projects receiving National Awards for Energy Innovation from the U.S. Department of Energy in 1991, and was one of two projects to receive an award from the State of Indiana for Energy Innovation in 1990.

Sociodemographic Characteristics—

Clearwater, Florida

1990 Population:

98,784

Median Age:

42.2

Household Composition:

74.1% in families

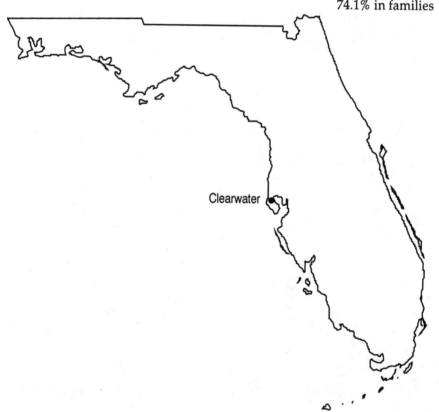

Chapter 2

The Long Center: A Comprehensive, Nonprofit Recreation Facility

Clearwater, Florida

Mark Abdo
Executive Director
The Long Center

I. The Situation

Nestled between Tampa Bay and the Gulf of Mexico, Pinellas County is Florida's smallest county as measured by square mileage, but it is home for the state's most dense population base. Most County land is urbanized or suburbanized, anchored by St. Petersburg in the south and Clearwater and Dunedin in the north, with twenty organized municipalities other than the larger cities. In anticipation of the growing demand for leisure services, a youth sports organization, Clearwater For Youth (CFY), was incorporated as a nonprofit 501(C)3 entity nearly three decades ago. CFY initially served several thousand youths throughout the Clearwater area utilizing volunteer coaches and private vehicles. CFY dreamed of a comprehensive facility with ample open space for playing fields they could call their own. For twenty years CFY leaders sought the financial assistance that would help the organization realize its dream.

Initially conceived solely as a Clearwater For Youth project, CFY gradually assumed a fundraising coordination role in addition to its original direct provider orientation. Therefore, CFY created the Center Foundation which ultimately became responsible for fundraising, building and operating the Center. The Foundation grew to incorporate a much larger scope of agencies and interests represented by the City of Clearwater Parks and Recreation Department, YWCA of Clearwater, Upper Pinellas Association of Retarded Citizens (UPARC), and the City of Safety Harbor Leisure Services. The centerpiece of this cooperative effort was the proposed facility—later named the Long Center in recognition of the generous contributions of Zip and Shirley Long. Each agency had unique reasons for becoming involved in the arrangement. For example, the UPARC home was several decades old and deteriorating and UPARC staff wanted to place their clients in an inclusive mainstream atmosphere. This coalition of agencies worked together to construct a comprehensive facility capable of providing services to meet their diverse needs.

II. Vision

The vision which evolved by the mid-1980s was to build a centrally-located, accessible facility which met all of the community's youth sports needs. Ideally, all youth wishing to participate would be able to do so without constraints related to access, physical or financial ability. The Clearwater For Youth Recreation Facility would consist of several baseball, football and soccer fields, a gymnasium, track, outdoor swimming pool, basketball and tennis courts. The basic concept was that a place provided for all kids to go, play hard, leave tired, and go home to sleep at night instead of being on the streets.

III. Objectives

The Center Foundation developed several objectives to guide construction and operation of the Long Center:

1. To provide a place where champions gather, including participants, spectators, special athletes and instructors.

2. To establish an endowment for operational expenses.

3. To position the Center as a friend within the community—a safe place for kids and adults of all ages.

4. To create a facility and programs conducive to bringing together developmentally handicapped participants with others.

5. To develop a cooperative and facilitative model for other recreation agencies and communities to emulate.

6. To encourage reciprocity between agency program fees which would allow higher use levels to lower per capita service provision costs.

7. To allow volunteers to become an integral part of operations.

IV. Management Paradigm Shift

The major internal paradigm shift for the Long Center was to operate the proposed facility as a business, distinct from the traditional operating patterns of many nonprofit leisure facilities. As a result of this decision, Long Center staff have responsibilities beyond the roles traditionally assumed by recreation programmers. For example, the Executive Director of the Long Center meets weekly with a full-time accountant to review operations from a financial perspective.

A second paradigm shift, which evolved over the course of the planning process, involved the decision that the Center would act primarily in a cooperative and facilitative fashion with numerous public agencies, nonprofit agencies and commercial businesses in order to deliver services to multiple constituencies effectively. For example, board representatives from government agencies vote on policymaking that affects financial and programming decisions of their agencies, but they do not have advisory powers within the Long Center.

Third, from the public sector's perspective, the decision to cooperate with the Long Center regarding leisure services provision also represented a major paradigm shift for several municipal government agencies that traditionally relied heavily or solely on direct provider delivery systems. Overall management and control of a facility by a private, nonprofit organization (Long Center) represented some loss of power and control over traditionally government-provided services.

Fourth, government representatives allowed business leaders to take initiatives that impacted public leisure services delivery. As a benefit, recreation agencies in several cities have access to a large-scale $15 million, mortgage-free facility—the Long Center. Thousands of visitors and potential customers have access to the facility due to reciprocal agreements with various partner agencies.

In summary, the Long Center concept represents a fundamental paradigm shift from the traditional, relatively isolated decision-making and programming processes carried out by individual recreation agencies. Perhaps the most telling descriptor of the Long Center's innovativeness is the inability of state-level governing bodies to monitor and regulate the Center's operations. The federal government (represented by the Internal Revenue Service) considers the Long Center to be a tax-free, nonprofit operation. However, due to the uniqueness of the Long Center's mission and operating procedures, the State of Florida does not recognize contributions to the facility as being tax-free under 501(C)3 Florida Code. According to the Code, the Long Center did not meet criteria for tax-free status because it provides a purely facilitative role and does not offer any direct recreation programming on its own. The Long Center recently made the decision to offer programming which complements the programs being offered by its partner agencies—a decision that may ease problems with the Florida 501(C)3 Code. Nevertheless, Long Center officials encouraged state tax officials to rework the current state codes to accommodate nonprofit facilities with interagency cooperative mandates.

V. Key Players

The list of key players involved in the Long Center project included a diverse array of private citizens and citizens representing several levels of government: the philanthropist and founder of Clearwater For Youth; the (now former) Center Foundation Executive Director; two former Governors of Florida; the past Clearwater City Manager; the former Safety Harbor City Manager; the Director of Clearwater Parks and Recreation; the Director of Safety Harbor Leisure Services; several Center Foundation Trustees; and the Executive Director of the Long Center.

VI. Processes Undertaken to Accomplish Change

Clearwater For Youth provided the initial idea for the Long Center project. In founder Fred Fisher, CFY had an individual with ample finances and sufficient available time to spearhead the project. Nevertheless, it took two decades of planning and consensus building before the project gained widespread acceptance. Momentum for construction of the Long Center facility gathered in the early 1980s. By this time, CFY leadership identified key supporters in the community and political supporters locally, statewide, and even at the national level. A community committee developed to gather input from local constituencies. Together with these opinion leaders and the input from local residents, CFY made a positive argument to the Clearwater City Commission that, if constructed, the Center would serve many of the recreational needs of Clearwater's residents. Support for the concept, also based on the City's comprehensive plan, showed growing demands for leisure services, and the proposed facility's potential to provide services at a lower cost to taxpayers. CFY partnered with the City of Clearwater in 1986. Shortly thereafter, in 1989, the State of Florida contributed $3 million to supplement the seed money already gathered for construction. The third permanent partner, UPARC, joined the partnership prior to facility construction.

The Center Foundation organized in September 1986 to raise funds and manage endowments associated with the proposed facility. The Center Foundation evolved because the original dream of CFY had grown and now included three other agencies which represented the state, a city, and another nonprofit organization. Sixty percent of capital finances came from the private sector, twenty percent came from the State of Florida, and twenty percent came from local governments. The City of Clearwater and the Center Foundation signed the first lease associated with the new facility.

The lease was quite standard with two exceptions. First, the City was charged monthly office rent based on a fee of $1.50 per square foot. Second, program fees paid to the Center were based on the previous year's program usage. This arrangement is made possible by differentiating the fiscal year from the use year or historical data report. Participant attendance figures for City of Clearwater programs are compiled in a fiscal year beginning on the first of March and running through the end of February. This calendar allows a grace period of one month for the Center to plug the numbers into their approved budget by the beginning of April for the upcoming fiscal years.

The Center Foundation acted as general contractor to save money on construction costs for early payments and sales tax while the Long Center was being built. The Center Foundation created the Long Center as the management company to operate the facility. The Center's current Executive Director began work in 1989. The center initially hired maintenance and aquatics personnel, records and membership personnel, a volunteer coordinator and an accountant. The Long Center began operations in July 1989. In addition to the outdoor facilities, previously listed in Section II, the Long Center also boasted space for indoor soccer and tennis, a three-court hardwood gymnasium, an adult fitness room, 75,000 square feet of classrooms, and indoor aquatic facilities. The Long Center's operations are separate from the operations of the Center Foundation whose sole purpose is to serve as the fundraising arm of the Long Center. Two additional partners joined the mix in 1989-1990: the City of Safety Harbor and the YWCA of Clearwater. However, the latter organization only stayed for eight months due to a merger with the St. Petersburg YWCA.

If communities as small as 15,000 people, such as Safety Harbor and many of the other small municipalities in Pinellas County, operated an independent park and recreation agency, as is the norm, they could not begin to construct, operate or support a facility as comprehensive in scope as the Long Center. Unlike the lease arrangement signed between the Long Center and the City of Clearwater, use agreements were drawn between the Long Center, the City of Safety Harbor, CFY and UPARC. Such sponsor agencies are assessed user fees based on the actual Long Center costs minus all sources of Long Center revenue. The two major contributors in this area are the cities of Clearwater (70 percent of residual costs) and Safety Harbor (25 percent of residual costs). This arrangement encourages member agencies to promote instructional classes and facility memberships because as these revenues increase, residual costs decrease. UPARC's unique use agreement involves the offices and classrooms used by their agency since they occupy 50 percent of the Center's square footage. Thus, UPARC is responsible for 50 percent of common expenses including groundskeepers' wages, perimeter lighting, common maintenance and building contracts.

The Joe DiMaggio Complex reinforced the Center Foundation's initial commitment to improve leisure facilities in the County. Located two miles from the Long Center on the campus of St. Petersburg Junior College (SPJC), the Complex includes two tournament-quality baseball diamonds and five soccer/football fields. Originally leased by the Center Foundation to the SPJC for $1 a year, the complex was recently sold to SPJC which is now responsible for maintaining and operating the facility. Under terms of the sale agreement, Long Center affiliated agencies retain priority use rights (after SPJC functions) and the Center Foundation has the right to name fields within the complex as a fundraising tool for major sponsors.

VII. Marketing to Internal and/or External Publics

The Long Center successfully manipulated numerous marketing mix variables to serve the people of Pinellas County. The plan evolved based on the Center's Mission Statement and long-range plan. The interagency cooperation initiated and organized by CFY established the long-term arrangement to transform many external constituencies, such as public recreation departments in Clearwater and Safety Harbor and nonprofit agencies such as UPARC and CFY, into internal constituencies. Organized opposition to the Long Center's initiatives has been negligible. The local business community provided a powerful voice to support the Long Center and the Center Foundation's other projects and programs. Careful planning enhanced the reputation of both the Center Foundation and the Long Center. Center planners visited other public and private leisure facilities operating in Florida to use them as models prior to facility construction. Long Center staff manipulated the full range of marketing mix variables (i.e., program/product development, distribution considerations, price strategies, and promotional efforts) to serve participants and other clients.

In addition to the opening of the Long Center and the Joe DiMaggio Complex, recent programming innovations include cooperative efforts with local corporations and hotels. Working with Innovative Leisure, Inc., a southern Florida company specializing in corporate picnics and special events, Long Center staff are currently investigating possibilities for making the Center a venue for many such gatherings. The Long Center recently entered into contract negotiations with Friday Nite Live, Inc., an alternative youth program for children ages nine to fourteen. Friday Nite Live offers many simultaneous activities for youth during weekend evenings. These programs offer a safe, fun place for kids and peace of mind for parents. By offering this community service, the Long Center also generates revenue during typically slow use periods. The physical facility is still evolving. For example, plans are being formulated to construct additional facilities on-site which include large gathering rooms, a track, indoor shuffleboard and hockey field.

Distribution related challenges are numerous for the Long Center. Its central location within the County makes it somewhat accessible to everyone, but like any facility, the best access is afforded to those who live close by. Thus, many important constituencies have not enjoyed the type of convenient access provided by smaller neighborhood facilities. These problems are gradually being addressed in a comprehensive manner. For example, the City of Clearwater recently completed a seven-mile long, east-west linear park, complete with a paved bicycle trail which begins (or ends, depending on the individual resident's perspective) at the Long Center. A new east-west oriented bus line commenced operation in July 1993 that provides ridership services directly to the Long Center every 90 minutes. This bus route serves residents of Clearwater and Safety Harbor.

Operating hours also fall under the rubric of distribution issues faced by the Long Center. Recent budget and participation analyses showed that the Center was underutilized. It was losing money on weekends and unable to meet the heavy demand for weekday services especially during early morning and early evening hours. Therefore, the decision to phase-in closing the Center on weekends, unless the facility is committed on a contractual basis, was made. The money saved would be used to expand weekday morning hours. As a result, the Center will be free to book special events on weekends. Sport-related rentals, such as baseball card shows, Junior Olympics, high school sporting events, college training programs, and international basketball teams, became very popular weekend events. The Center focuses on all levels of competitive sports and training-related events.

Pricing decisions are determined in large part by budgetary decisions of major partners such as the City of Clearwater. One problem that is still being worked out is the low priority that Long Center funding receives from communities which consider its programs to be adjunct services. Participating communities have a vested interest in the Center's self-sufficiency since fees for use agreements are determined by the financial needs of the Center above and beyond its earned income. The Long Center offers scholarship programs for potential participants unable to pay user fees. (Initially the facility was developed for youth but it also has a large adult user population.) Many scholarship recipients are referred by participating municipal agencies, and the Center Foundation itself recommends many of the potential scholarship recipients. Nonscholarship participants learn about the program through published brochures.

Promotion efforts are characterized by personal communication used to educate potential constituents about the purpose and function of the Long Center and Center Foundation, and their interrelationship with affiliated agencies and businesses. A video titled "The Place Where Other Champions Gather" is presented to professional organizations and service clubs in Pinellas County. The Long Center continues its regular practice of offering discussions and presentations to area parks and recreation departments, and the Center's staff regularly contributes to Florida Recreation and Park Association (FRPA) meetings.

The Long Center has a volunteer, but professional, marketing committee that organized during the outset of the Center and plays a major role in cultivating positive publicity. They offered hard hat tours during the construction of the Center and published regular news articles highlighting fundraising successes, new staff appointments and construction highlights. Center staff also solicited and published written endorsements from national and state leaders. One constant theme stressed to participating agencies and communities is that shared usage is the way of the future. Staff members develop detailed financial models to graphically depict potential capital and operational savings to agencies. Special events were also helpful in generating early publicity. Examples include the "Help Fill the Pool—A Buck a Gallon" campaign and the "Dry Water Ballet" held on the Center's grounds before the official opening. The Long Center's grand opening celebration featured well-known Olympic athletes like Tracy Caulkins in attendance, carnival games, tours, an on-site membership drive, free use of the facilities, various program booths, and class registrations. Ongoing promotional efforts include cable television commercials made possible by more than $1,000,000 in cable sponsorship contributions, and continued nurturing of media relationships based on the concept that the Long Center is a unique facility, a jewel to the community, and a tourist attraction.

VIII. Impact of Change on the Agency

Operations changed dramatically following the opening ceremonies for the Long Center. Long Center attendance has been solid. During its first fifteen months of operation, more than 827,700 participants visited the facility (the first year's attendance goal was surpassed within six months). Attendance increased to more than 889,500 in the second fiscal year, and to over 939,000 in the third year. Spectator attendance is not included within these participation figures. The Center receives financial assistance from the Convention and Visitors Bureau to help bring larger events to the area. These developments increased the complexity of the Long Center's operations in comparison to the years before the facility opened. Committees of volunteers consisting of high-level professionals develop and administer policy related to marketing, building and grounds, personnel and finance. The Long Center benefited from an average of more than 15,000 volunteer hours per year since its inception.

The public profile of the Long Center also elevated. National and state political figures tour, major sport athletes visit and train at the facility, and fundraisers have been conducted by Mark Spitz and Karen and Sarah Josephson. The Long Center continues to serve as a major interagency facilitator in Pinellas County. Agency staff from many communities now work with each other for common goals, and therefore, assist each other with events, human resources, and planning.

IX. Impact of Change on the Communities

Most residents in Pinellas County communities perceive the Long Center to be a fitness and athletic club available for public use at a reasonable cost; this pleases the residents about their investments. Because the Long Center operates like a business, participating agencies and Center staff must account for their actions. Earned income brought in by the Long Center keeps agency funding minimal. In 1992-1993, the Long Center's earned income accounted for over $467,000 (54 percent of the facility's total revenue); Center Foundation contributions accounted for $140,000 (16 percent of the total revenue), and sponsor agencies contributed over $261,000 (30 percent of the total revenue).

Revenues realized from tourists increase as the number of large events hosted by the Long Center grow. The Center impacts the planning processes of cooperating agencies. For example, the County transit system included the facility in its master plan for a Clearwater/Safety Harbor bus route which began operation in 1993.

X. Measurement of the Outcome

The $15 million capital campaign achieved before the Center opened provided commentary regarding the effectiveness of this joint partnership, and, more specifically, the Center Foundation's financial planning efforts. However, adequate operating budgets must be made annually. The Long Center receives feedback regarding its efficiency and effectiveness from internal constituencies through the budget process undertaken each year by both city commissions. Overall attendance and financial figures are positive which results in lower total residual fees paid by participating agencies each year. Commercial sector corporate donors also conduct periodic reviews of the return on their investments from Long Center donations. Since its opening, the Long Center serves as an example of an efficient local public facility.

Tangible progress is more easily measured in competitive settings than in other program areas. For example, the local swim team moved from the fifteenth place standing to second in the State in the past several years, suggesting the modern indoor facility and positive atmosphere created at the Long Center generated interest and commitment among the County's young swimmers. User satisfaction is more difficult to measure. Feedback regarding program effectiveness is also gathered from peers and partners in participating and outside agencies, focus groups comprised of randomly chosen program participants, and from commentary on the Center's newsletter and quarterly volunteer forums. The marketing committee collects data related to variables such as the distances people travel to use the facility and reasons for purchasing memberships. The Executive Director and staff members are also charged with producing an annual "State of the Long Center" report. Stories featuring the Center recently published in two professional publications, include a story on the Dry Water Ballet program in the May 1990 issue of *Athletic Business*, and an article detailing the Long Center's innovative financing plan ran in the December 1992 issue of *Parks and Recreation*.

Author's Suggested Readings and References

Abdo, M. (1992). Financing recreation complexes for the future. *Parks and Recreation, 27*(12), pp. 26-29, 66-67.

Athletic Business Spirit Awards: The Center Foundation, Inc. (May 1990). *Athletic Business*, pp. 43-45.

Sociodemographic Characteristics—

Indianapolis

Indianapolis, Indiana

1990 Population:

731,327

Median Age:

31.6

Household Composition:

78.9% in families

Chapter 3

Leadership on Environmental Issues: Policy in Practice

Indianapolis, Indiana

Rob Corbett
Stewardship, Grants and Property Manager
Indianapolis Department of Parks and Recreation

I. The Situation

The situation driving this change model is not a problem unique to Indianapolis, Indiana. To the contrary, land development policies in Indianapolis are typically American. The policies featured construction of land-intensive subdivisions; planned developments designed to create quiet neighborhoods that, by design, force residents to drive ten minutes to get to stores located several hundred yards beyond their back fences; and ever expanding two-lane, four-lane, and six-lane highway systems to move people to and from the central city to their increasingly distant residences. In the midst of this reality, businesses, individuals, public and private agencies try to make intelligent land-use decisions.

Park and recreation departments serving large American cities typically are responsible for maintaining, developing and protecting large tracts of land. The Indianapolis Department of Parks and Recreation is no exception. It is responsible for more than 10,000 acres of parkland at over 300 different sites. Most of this property is held in fee simple by the Department, although it also has rights to many easements, and leases a diverse array of property from other agencies. Leased properties are a diverse lot ranging from river flood plains to school rooms and parking facilities. As a result of its land-intensive mandate, the Department deals regularly with multiple constituencies and interest groups including schools, other local, state and federal public agencies, business interests, real estate developers, neighborhood associations, activity-specific organizations (e.g., bicycle clubs, nature enthusiasts), and international organizations such as the Audubon Society and Sierra Club.

After many years of wrangling on park development issues, this diverse mix of government and citizen environmental groups grew to distrust one another to the point that communication about important matters was generally conflict-ridden. Emotional pleas, ultimatums, and alarmist tactics became the common tools of negotiation. Based on past experience, these groups distrusted the City government's ability to fulfill its role as land steward by developing facilities in a resource-sensitive manner, or managing natural areas to maintain their highest ecological potential. Without a policy to guide land stewardship decision making, the Department (referred to hereafter as Indy Parks) would make its "best call" and attempt to react to the often subjective and emotional criticisms of groups opposed to particular projects.

II. Vision

The vision was threefold. First, it urged that a policy guiding land management decisions be developed to empower all levels of park staff to make sound decisions on development, use, and management issues where land stewardship principles are a part of the equation. Second, Indy Parks desired that the citizen environmental groups, with which they deal regularly, approve of the policy. Third, it was hoped that the policy's terminology would reduce conflicts by supporting the use of objective and rational arguments, as opposed to subjective and emotional opinions, in a value-based decision-making process.

III. Objectives

Indy Parks developed the following four objectives:

1. To change the Department's often reactive positioning and place Indy Parks in a leadership role regarding environmental issues affecting the community. Department staff envisioned the creation of a forum where people could come to air concerns and work out problems before the Department drafted policies.

2. To create a foundation upon which Indy Parks, user groups, and citizen environmental groups could cooperate with community education by developing long-range plans and solving specific short-range problems.

3. To create a higher level of environmental ethics in all people's thought processes, so that policy development players from ball diamond advocates to landscape architects to real estate developers would try to envision proposals through other people's eyes. As a result, the site development process would become more sensitive over time as alternative perspectives would be more often considered up front.

4. To draft a policy that would actually contain the planning tools to effectively remedy conflicts involving land management questions rather than simply recommending that tools be created. That is, the policy would be authoritative rather than advisory in nature.

IV. Management Paradigm Shift

One important paradigm shift involved removing traditional bureaucratic barriers and "turfism" that hindered team decision making in-house in order to emphasize informed consent among various public employees and agencies. The process began by removing in-house barriers through an environmental review process which allows maintenance staff, planners, programmers and others to share input (and responsibility) in developing decisions about the environmental implications of the Department's work. This paradigm shift represented an example of redefining jobs, and empowerment for nonmanagerial employees.

A second shift involved the opening of policy and planning arenas to a broader public base through site visits, advisory boards, and other venues allowing people to bring their ideas (and eventually their endorsement) into the process before any plan reached its final stage.

Both of these management paradigm shifts represent an effort on the part of senior-level Department staff to delegate some measure of authority and initiative to groups that traditionally had little influence in resource management decisions.

V. Key Players

The chaos surrounding resource policy development concerned the members of the Indy Parks staff. Some of the initial impetus for change came from external sources such as National Recreation and Parks Association (NRPA) leadership that previously drafted a recommended environmental policy. Indy Parks also consulted with other park and recreation agencies, such as Lake Metroparks (Ohio) whose natural resource policies were a significant contribution. Indy Parks also sought local input from a comprehensive group of concerned individuals and agencies as detailed in Section VI of this chapter.

VI. Processes Undertaken to Accomplish Change

Indy Parks' Executive Director, who was hired in the spring of 1992, suggested a review of land development procedures. This initiative led staff to examine NRPA's report on environmental policy, consult with other park and recreation agencies, and create the position of Stewardship, Grants, and Property Manager which was filled in the fall of 1992. At this point, policy development began in earnest.

Leaders from Indianapolis' most active environmental groups and local land developers were asked to create and rank a comprehensive list of environmental issues so that it may be addressed by Indy Parks. Later the environmental groups and local land developers condensed the 33 issues to a shorter list of eight by combining similar issues. These issues, identified in Table 2, became guides for connecting public issues to policy actions. They represented a composite of common complaints (e.g., issues 3, 6, 7, and 8) and new initiatives resulted from the City's willingness to listen.

Many components of the Indy Parks initiatives, including the greenways plan, environmental education, wetlands protection and mowing reductions, were directly supported in the citizen-generated list. This correlation squelched claims of many skeptics who felt that the City was opening Pandora's box by inviting citizen input. The citizen-generated list allowed Indy Parks to proceed in clearly defined areas with the knowledge that they had the support of the community. It also provided a safety net against after-the-fact claims by groups and individuals who would claim there wasn't an opportunity for citizen input. Communication served as the City's "insurance policy" and kept dialogue open.

Environmental groups reviewed and commented on the policy eight times before the final draft was passed by the Indy Parks Board. Indy Parks' Stewardship, Grants and Property Manager developed all drafts of the policy and negotiated modifications with staff and citizen representatives. Implementation of the policy through an environmental project review process, ongoing natural resources inventory, and management plan development are now the responsibility of the Stewardship Section.

The draft policy was reviewed by both in-house staff and citizens between September and December of 1992. Board approval came in January of 1993 with an official announcement in the Mayor's press conference at the Indianapolis Open Space Workshop. Most Indy Parks staff became involved through the environmental review process as projects came into question through February and March. Guidelines were distributed, and on-the-job training site visits were used to educate staff on the policy and process.

Individual environmental policy review teams developed for each specific situation as it arose. For example, Indy Parks took on fifteen capital improvement projects in 1993, therefore fifteen review teams convened. Review teams consisted of a core group of internal Departmental representatives and

Table 2: Eight Land Stewardship Issues

1. Wetlands should be better managed and protected.

2. Greenways should be established along the county's major rivers and streams to create linkages.

3. There must be greater emphasis on environmental education in park programming and more outreach to schools.

4. Natural resource inventories and management plans should guide park facility development and prevent habitat loss.

5. The Parks and Recreation Department should develop a comprehensive open space protection plan.

6. Greater public involvement in park planning should be accommodated.

7. A comprehensive city-wide tree ordinance should be passed to protect urban trees.

8. The Parks and Recreation Department should play an active role in the zoning process to keep developers from filling and dredging wetlands and violating tree preservation commitments.

outside representatives as needed or requested. Team sizes ranged from four to fifteen members. The internal core group generally includes representatives from maintenance, recreation, or environmental interpretation, forestry, stewardship, planning and design, and special populations. Outside representatives may include: Indiana Department of Natural Resources (InDNR), philanthropic foundations, other city divisions (e.g., public works, transportation, real estate services), environmental organizations, businesses, and private citizens.

VII. Marketing to Internal and/or External Publics

Internal marketing efforts were relatively minimal since Departmental staff were included in the policy's development from the outset. Initially, some opposition arose from some old-guard members of the Indy Parks staff and their external supporters. However, opposition never went beyond occasional sniping for three reasons. The first reason involved the overwhelming community sentiment for change due to frustration with confrontational attitudes and gridlock. Second, the proposed policy reflected a positive, rather than negative, perspective. The policy presented not as "we have to change," but instead as "here is a vision of what we can be and here is one way that we can achieve the vision." Third, few staff members opposed the project, although many initially showed indifference. One goal of the policy was to empower nonadministrators. The attitudes of most staff changed dramatically once they were brought to a site and asked, "What would you do about this problem?" For example, a trails project had generated few initial comments from Indy Parks' staff. However, when the review team visited the site for a 45-minute meeting on a cold, rainy December day, the visit turned into an all-day affair as people's enthusiasm increased because of their input in the project.

Anticipated hostility between city staff and representatives from various state agencies never materialized. Traditionally city-state government relations were strained since different political parties dominated city and state politics. One example of cooperation between these groups was the suggestion by an out-of-state review team member to explore a federal wetlands management program administered by the U.S. Fish and Wildlife Service as a mechanism for preserving wetlands near or on school properties. This suggestion resulted in four successful projects and a pledge of continued cooperation from the Fish and Wildlife Service on future Indy Parks open space projects.

External marketing efforts were also characterized by heavy levels of personal contact between Indy Parks staff and external constituencies. The external constituencies became directly involved in the program planning and policy development processes.

Throughout the process, the active environmental groups involved in Indy Parks issues were invited to give input. On January 15, 1993, the "Indianapolis Open Space Workshop" introduced the Land Stewardship policy to the community. Speakers at the workshop focused on strategies that could enable the policy and/or be enabled by the policy. Real estate professionals, attorneys, developers, and others not ordinarily involved in promoting environmental improvements participated in this workshop.

Future plans involve personal contact, and feature input by participants as important components of the marketing and promotion mixes. The format for this information exchange process is continuing to evolve. Initially, the Natural Resources Advisory Council formed by members from the academic community, related government agencies and members of environmental groups to provide regular input on implementation of the policy. However, that Council disbanded after a short time in favor of an informal process modeled after the Department's in-house environmental review process whereby committees are formed on an ad hoc basis as the need for specific reviews arise. The former Council's outward appearance of a "star chamber" for only the most vocal eco-elitist members of the community could have hindered open dialogue. The project-by-project review process allows for better input from a wider range of individuals and groups. More detail and commitment is also apparent because the "seldom-asked" people tend to treat matters with both honesty and seriousness of purpose.

A series of informational publications was produced in the spring of 1994 to enhance public understanding and participation in adoption-type programs wherein community or neighborhood groups "adopt" a specific park or section of park for the purpose of performing maintenance or improving habitat. These publications were distributed through the zoning, planning, and permitting offices of the city as well as through Indy Parks Stewardship and customer service. In April 1994 the Indianapolis Conference on Empowerment, Environment and Economics (E³) further involved professionals, citizens and user groups in the implementation of the policy beyond the scope of lands controlled by Indy Parks. The conference featured three learning tracks: Stream Corridor Restoration, Tax Deductions for Private Land Protection, and Greenways: Managing the Community Input Process. In addition to educating participants regarding open-space policy issues, the conference raised general public awareness and enhanced the credibility of the Indianapolis land stewardship policy initiative.

The E³ Conference was based on the three themes in its title. The *economics* component focused on tax benefits for protecting private land, environmental enhancements to reduce the cost of doing business, and environmentally sensitive development as a marketing tool for developers. The *empowerment* component emphasized the *a priori* involvement of community planning teams before government planners designed the project, and adoption-type (adopt-a-park) projects that involve the public in planning and programming open space while saving tax dollars. The *environment* component articulated how the environment directly impacts future land-use choices, how it is related to economic and empowerment issues, and how a healthy environment represents a desirable condition regardless of emotional and other subjective concerns.

VIII. Impact of Change on the Agency

This policy has only recently taken effect. However, three areas of expected impact involve staff productivity, staff efficiency, and staff morale. Productivity should improve because environmental concerns will be addressed up front in the planning, maintenance and programming functions. Past experience suggested that retrofitting environmental needs after the fact is a time consuming and costly procedure.

Efficiency will certainly increase as some open-space areas are removed from the mowing schedules, nuisance species (such as bush honeysuckle and multiflora rose) are controlled, and waste is reduced thereby allowing maintenance hours to be directed toward enhancement of active-use areas. One of the review teams created under the new policy is charged specifically with monitoring the Department's mowing schedule in response to maintenance division budget constraints. The review team consists of a landscape architect, a member of the mowing crew, a U.S. Fish and Wildlife Service representative, an Indiana Department of Natural Resources representative, a student intern, and the Stewardship Manager. The team examines each park individually to decide where mowing can be reduced or eliminated. Recently the review team proposed recommendations for the first park that changed 84 acres of mowed land into meadow and oldfield management resulting in an estimated $6,000 annual savings in maintenance costs. It is hoped that their proposed solutions will not only save the Department money, but will also improve wildlife habitat and visitor enjoyment. Another team, consisting of interpretive staff, a student intern, a InDNR representative, and a Fish and Wildlife representative, works on prairie and wildflower restoration projects in several parks which will also reduce mowing pressures.

Though it is too early to claim conclusively, it is expected that morale will be improved since fear of the unknown is reduced through line-staff involvement in the planning and evaluation process. One of the most influential members of the environmental review process is a seventeen-year veteran of the park maintenance staff (mowing crew) who began planting hardwoods in some open parkland during the Arab oil embargo. No recognition of this person's added effort was noted at the time. However, the employee's actions contributed to beautifying the parks and eliminated the need to mow substantial acreage. Under the new environmental land use policy, he is recognized as the Department's forest reclamation expert while providing a classic example of job enrichment.

IX. Impact of Change on the Community

Two changes of note have occurred to date. First, participation by environmental groups, user groups, and others became more frequent and much less confrontational. Admittedly there is still mistrust to overcome, but through continual participation in the environmental review process this problem should continue to diminish. Particular success evolved through involving environmental groups in the natural resource inventory process; the groups contributed the data they gathered in pursuit of their pastimes. For example, the Nature Sanctuary and Center, Inc., a local nonprofit organization primarily comprised of school teachers and nature enthusiasts from throughout the county, work closely with stewardship maintenance staff at Eagle Creek Park.

The nonprofit group adopted some basic maintenance duties (many carried out by students in environmental education classes) at the north end of this large natural park, thus freeing up maintenance staff to concentrate its limited staff resources on maintenance of active recreation areas. An additional benefit of this arrangement allows maintenance staff to be better aware of the outcomes desired by environmental educators and birders.

Customer service improved. Inquiries about Indy Parks' policy on land stewardship issues is now met with definitive answers, and citizens are invited into the act through adoption programs that promote the policy. Residents are better informed about environmental issues that affect the park system. On average, the Stewardship division fields between 50 and 70 phone inquiries per week on various issues. Some highly visible issues, such as the Park Capital Improvements Plan, accounted for four or five calls per hour over extended periods of time. Department staff noted that the nature of most phone calls changed. Presently, most calls are from people interested in procuring information, whereas previous calls were dominated by negative responses to proposed projects.

X. Measurement of the Outcome

Citizen inquiries are monitored from initial contact through to completion. Inquiries that are satisfied without referrals are considered successful. The desired outcome is a more informed public which understands the needs for proper land stewardship. Referred inquiries are monitored to determine the Park Staff's level of knowledge when addressing land stewardship issues. Inappropriately directed referrals that reflect misinformation are used to target areas where inculcation of in-house staff is required. The desired outcome is a consistent representation of policy to the public with reduced disparity in information given out by the department's staff.

Indy Parks' staff were concerned that the review process not become too bureaucratic in nature. Therefore, environmental reviews of projects under the capital improvements plan are assessed by how quickly a submitted project results in a completed review. For example, given the number of projects planned in 1993, a target time period of three weeks was considered successful. The first pilot project for environmental policy, conducted at Indianapolis' historic and high profile Holliday Park, was completed in four weeks. The desired outcome for smooth incorporation of environmental concerns in the planning process reduces the need to retrofit projects at the midpoint.

Park adoptions and volunteerism are considered successes. When individual citizens or groups choose to become involved in implementation of a policy, that policy is considered a success. The desired outcome increased trust and citizen involvement in the Department's efforts. The Nature

Sanctuary and Center project in Eagle Creek Park is one example. Another includes relationships with nonprofit organizations (e.g., Friends of Holliday Park, the Central Indiana Bicycle Association).

Inventory of park natural resources must be a primary measure. A target of four park areas for inventory work in 1993 was set. Completion of inventory on three areas with a minimum level of 30 percent volunteer and student intern involvement constituted a successful year. The desired outcome is efficient production of planning data before management policies and improvements are initiated.

Author's Suggested Readings and References

Cronon, W. (1983). *Changes in the land: Indians, colonists, and the ecology of New England.* New York, NY: Hill and Wang.

Environmental Review Process: For Land Acquisitions and Developments. Indy Parks and Recreation, Division of Natural Resources Stewardship Section.

Land Stewardship Policy: Governing Lands Under the Jurisdiction of Indy Parks and Recreation. Indy Parks and Recreation, Division of Natural Resources Stewardship Section.

Miller, D. R. (n.d.) *Mow maintenance assessments of Eagle Creek Park.* Unpublished manuscript, Indianapolis Department of Parks and Recreation.

Sociodemographic Characteristics—

Kansas City, Missouri

1990 Population:

435,146

Median Age:

32.7

Household Composition:

77.7% in families

● Kansas City

Chapter 4

Successful and Effective Contracting of Maintenance Services

Kansas City, Missouri

Steve Lampone
Superintendent of Parks
Department of Parks and Recreation

I. The Situation

Many American cities experienced years of post World War II economic expansion in which public sector agencies shared slices of ever larger budget pies. Until the mid-1980s, public agencies commonly provided their own services rather than seek alternative service delivery methods. Shrinking municipal budgets, common in the 1980s, forced some agencies to reevaluate direct provider policies in many communities. Although Kansas City's Department of Parks and Recreation did not experience budget limitations common in today's environment as quickly, the availability of resources began to change radically in the past few years. As a result, Kansas City's park maintenance managers face a host of problematic situations in the 1990s, some common to those currently faced in all U.S. cities and some unique to Kansas City. These challenges prompted the Department of Parks and Recreation to initiate alternative service delivery strategies. Problems and challenges associated with the Kansas City Department of Parks and Recreation's traditional direct provider approach follow.

The first problem involves actual reductions in government spending. Kansas City's General Fund support for the Department of Parks and Recreation decreased from $3.8 million in 1985 to $1.7 million in 1990. However, prior to 1991 modest budget increases continued due to funding from other sources which showed an overall increase. The Kansas City Parks and Recreation budget peaked in 1991 at $6.5 million, but decreased over the past several years to $6.3 million annually.

The second challenge includes the rising costs of labor, equipment, and materials which complicates budget reductions. Because the minimum wage of $4.35/hour paid to seasonal part-time staff is not competitive, it is difficult for the Department to fill positions. The Department's part-time work force has been, in general, poorly educated and, in some cases, poorly motivated.

Unemployment costs were also problematic because of the Department's financial responsibility to former employees even though many worked only six months per year.

The third problem concerns aging facilities and equipment which are commonplace in Kansas City. Kansas City uses many Works Progress Administration (WPA) and Civilian Conservation Corps (CCC) facilities built in the 1930s. These old facilities contain inefficient heating and cooling systems—common elements within such old buildings.

Problems caused by budget shortfalls and aging infrastructure were exacerbated by the demand for more and better services. For example, the Kansas City Zoo attracted 250,000 visitors in 1985 whereas 1995 visitor projections are in the 750,000 to 1,000,000 range. In a 1989 Kansas City citizen survey, 90 percent of the respondents requested additional park and recreation services, but only 23 percent favored increasing taxes to pay for these additional services. Donated parkland also increased demands on park maintenance staff, even though maintenance endowments equal to 25 percent of the assessed value of the land are required from all land donations.

As a prelude to overhauling park development and maintenance practices, Kansas City's Department of Parks and Recreation surveyed staffs from other U.S. parks departments regarding their involvement in contractual services. The surveys revealed that in 1975, state and local agency contractual purchases for goods and services amounted to $36 billion, or 24 percent of their total expenditures. By 1984 the percentage rose to an estimated 30 percent of expenditures. Further, the 1985 survey indicated that departments in 59 percent of responding cities transferred at least some public services to the private sector. Parks and recreation agencies contracted for the following services most often: (a) operation and management of special facilities (e.g., ice skating rinks, tennis complexes, golf courses); (b) cooperative use agreements with school districts; and (c) design and construction of recreation facilities. Kansas City historically contracted out services in the latter two areas. For example, the City recently hired private contractors to build five new community centers for an estimated cost of $2.5 million each.

The Department's 1992 survey revealed that relatively few agencies (about 20 percent) had been involved in providing park maintenance services on a contractual basis. The same survey indicated an overwhelming majority (86 percent) of departments planned to either initiate (27 percent), maintain (18 percent), or increase (41 percent) the number and scope of contracted maintenance services. Fewer than two percent of responding agencies planned to decrease contracted maintenance activity and twelve percent were undecided. However, contractual agreements are not a panacea. Although the Department's cooperative ventures with school districts benefit both organizations, schedule conflicts and prioritization problems often arise. Care must be taken to develop contractual agreements that do not cause more problems than they solve.

II. Vision

Kansas City's Parks and Recreation staff envisioned a situation where the Department would operate at peak efficiency with respect to park maintenance. Management and union representatives negotiated a maximum level of allowable contracting that would allow the City to train traditional maintenance employees better, and allow greater flexibility in assignments. These changes are designed to remove skilled city employees from routine tasks related to mowing and trimming, and allow them to concentrate on fountain maintenance and masonry work instead.[1]

III. Objectives

The Kansas City Parks and Recreation Department developed the following eight objectives:

1. *Develop closer ties with neighborhood and community groups.* The Department developed facilitative arrangements with several neighborhood associations whereby the associations subcontract park maintenance tasks using City funds. This policy acts as incentive for neighborhood residents to develop a sense of stewardship in their parks. They add their own volunteer time and effort to the resources supplied by the Department, and further enhance the overall appearance of the parks.

2. *Curb the rising cost and size of government.* Rather than assume that contracted services are less expensive than City provided services, the program allows for comparison of costs incurred by both public and private sector maintenance crews. The Department monitors costs closely from both groups.

3. *Provide services that may be beyond the skills of the existing in-house labor force* (e.g., electrical and plumbing needs, irrigation installation and repair).

4. *Increase the flexibility of the existing labor force.* Skilled city employees are freed for more challenging tasks when they are not limited to routine duties.

---

[1] These are not minor tasks given the scale of Kansas City's investment in fountains and boulevards. Kansas City is recognized as having more fountains than any city in the world, save Rome, Italy, and it ranks second to Paris, France, in miles of boulevards. Construction and maintenance responsibility for these important landmarks and resources traditionally rests with the Department of Parks and Recreation.

5. *Support the private sector.* In addition to local contractors, local suppliers of maintenance equipment and chemicals can benefit from this program.

6. *Develop a business constituency that supports parks and recreation and, in particular, the Department.* Many maintenance contractors become effective supporters of the Department of Parks and Recreation in municipal bond and levy elections.

7. *Avoid the purchase or rental of costly equipment that is used on a limited basis.* Seldom used equipment such as tree spades, drill seeders, and other complex, breakdown-prone equipment (e.g., street sweepers) can be contracted from private landscape companies.

8. *Shift some Worker's Compensation and General Liability Insurance costs to independent contractors.* Theoretically, all private bids include these costs, but the amount of expenditures on Parks and Recreation full-time employees far exceeds the incremental increase included in individual bids.

IV. Management Paradigm Shift

The paradigm shift involved changing the mind-sets of Parks and Recreation Department administrators, union officials, and employees to recognize that private sector involvement in the provision of some maintenance services might benefit all entities and constituencies involved.

V. Key Players

Four individuals within the Parks Division initiated the change including the Director of Parks and Recreation, the Park Superintendent, and two of the four District Managers.

VI. Processes Undertaken to Accomplish Change

The change process, formally initiated in 1986, followed several years of informal discussion based on the premise that contracting could save the Department money in some situations.

Cost comparisons. The first stage in developing an effective contract system involves conducting accurate cost comparisons of in-house services versus contracted services. Agencies cannot be intimidated by cost comparisons if contractual programs are to be successful. At least four characteristics of commercial businesses often give private contractors distinct advantages over public sector agencies in this context.

First, private operators generally have lower personnel costs. For example, the Kansas City Department is mandated to provide cost of living allowances (COLA) to employees based on prior union negotiations; not so with most small businesses.

Second, private employers face fewer regulations and limitations regarding personnel decisions. Managers of City Departments sometimes are limited by regulations regarding the assignment of certain types of jobs to certain employees.

Third, private contractors enjoy greater flexibility in day-to-day operations. They often are not required to complete purchase orders and can, therefore, purchase equipment and supplies without restriction.

Fourth, specialization permits economies of scale. For example, a construction contractor may do curb and gutter work, and thus, use a pouring form regularly, whereas the Park and Recreation Department would have fewer occasions to use such equipment.

However, public sector agencies should not accept this discussion as fact without conducting their own analysis. Agencies must develop work programs and budgets for all maintenance programs currently being provided in-house. Most departments only have vague ideas about program costs because of inadequate cost accounting procedures. It is essential that agencies determine their own in-house costs as accurately as possible. At least five variables should be included in this analysis:

1. All direct labor costs including wages, salaries, and overtime;

2. Clerical and other support costs;

3. Training and licensing costs;

4. Other operating costs which involve service delivery (e.g., liability insurance, uniforms, equipment maintenance and repair); and,

5. Equipment depreciation attributable to each service or program.

Following this internal audit, parks and recreation agencies should attempt to determine contract costs for those programs and services that could potentially be done by outside agencies and businesses. Again, five variables should be considered:

1. *Direct payments to the contractor for services rendered.* These costs usually vary depending on situational factors. For example, mowing costs are not equally spread over warm-weather

seasons, but instead are dependent on other variables such as rainfall levels. Accordingly, the contracting agency should develop a range of estimates for all contracts.

2. *Costs involved in preparing contracts and writing specifications.* Revisions, though usually minor, are generally necessary each year.

3. *Costs involved for supervising and administering contracts during the course of a year.*

4. *Cost for developing and administering alternative plans* if the contractor fails to carry the project or service to completion in a satisfactory manner.

5. *Costs for bid advertisement and promotion.*

A sample cost comparison developed by the Kansas City Department is shown in Appendix A (page 169).

The key questions which must be answered relate to the amount of revisions that are necessary each year, and whether the administrative costs of developing and monitoring contracts are so restrictive as to negate any potential initial savings. In addition, it is important that agency administrators consider situational factors. The Kansas City Department of Parks and Recreation identified several situations in which the benefits of contracting generally outweigh the risks.

First, contracting is effective when travel time and costs can be saved by addressing maintenance in isolated or outlying areas. The City auditor considers travel time nonproductive. These situations are relatively common in Kansas City because its 10,000 acres of parkland is spread over a large (316 square miles) geographical area. Based on the U.S. city average of approximately 1,000 people per square mile, Kansas City's nearly 450,000 people would live in an area about 225 square miles instead.

Second, as noted earlier, contracting is preferred when specialized skills or equipment for a job will likely be underutilized by a department over the long-term. It is also effective when short-term needs prevail, or when additional assistance is necessary during heavier seasonal periods. This scenario became more common in recent years as fewer seasonal staff exist on the Department's payroll. Contracting is preferred to test new technology, or when equipment obsolescence is probable. For example, the City evaluated new mowers by monitoring their performance in the equipment fleets of contractors. Likewise, the Department required a contractor to use a non-2-4-D herbicide and evaluate its performance in a test-market type situation. Although generally not a problem faced by large cities such as Kansas City, contracting may be an appropriate option for smaller agencies that cannot justify expenditures for employees and equipment in specialized situations.

Finally, the most effective contracting happens when the need for public contact is minimal. Departmental experience suggests that City employees handle public contact better than contracted employees do. However, some contact is inevitable because most citizens assume that all employees, including contractors, are City employees. As a result, Kansas City's park maintenance contracts specify that contracted employees must wear uniforms and respond to citizens' complaints and comments within certain parameters.

Contract feasibility (noncost issues). The first concern to be considered is the agency's ability to contract services. The following issues must be addressed:

- Union contracts;
- Sentiments of the agency's governing body;
- Legal restrictions;
- Community receptivity;
- Available alternatives; and,
- Additional impacts on agency.

An investigation into alternative methods of service provision revealed at least two options other than private sector involvement. The first suggestion was to reduce the level of maintenance provided—an option that was unacceptable to the general public. The second, involving a shift of resources from within the Department, was determined to be too damaging to other park programs.

Meetings with union officials as well as the rank and file members of the AFSCME local were scheduled *prior* to the implementation of the program. The Department gave assurances that the primary objective of the program involved upgrading the maintenance of the park system as well as increasing the promotability of the current work force through reassignment to more skilled and complex jobs.

Contract development. Numerous issues must be considered at this stage in the process. First, Department staff must identify work activities to be contracted using the process described above. After suitable work activities are selected for contracting, it is important to conduct a complete inventory to determine the total number of units in the system. Units might be defined in terms of acreage, facilities, equipment, or other relevant variables. When inventorying actual park acreage, it is essential that legal surveys be utilized. If legal documentation is not used, future disagreements between the government agency and the contractor as to the number of contracted acres are a real possibility. Third, staff must determine the desired service level. At this point, it becomes possible to develop a sound set of specifications.

In addition to reflecting the level of service selected, specifications must be complete, concise and enforceable. This is not problematic in Kansas City, partially because contracts get better every year. Contracts should define all potentially ambiguous terms. For example, Kansas City's contracts explicitly define terms such as production rate, inclement weather, maintenance cycle, and grounds maintenance project areas. Particularly important common terms (e.g., trash, litter) are also defined in order to minimize potential confusion and misunderstandings. Contracts must answer questions of who, what, where, and when work is to be performed. Appendix A (pages 170-171) outlines Kansas City's contractor maintenance specifications. Kansas City segments potential contracts by size and scope, and by geographic location within the city. This practice allows contractors of various sizes and resources to successfully compete for different jobs, and allows region-based contractors economies related to time and travel if they restrict their bids to contracts for specific areas of the City.

Contracts should clarify special skills or expertise required, detail expected appearance of the contractor's on-site employees, and specify cleanup expected of contractors. Finally, contracts must list potential damage against which to guard, identify situations which pose health or safety hazards to park users and instructions on how to avoid the situations, and should detail expected level of communication or contact between the agency and contractor.

Extra care should also be taken when determining payment methods. This issue can affect the quality, quantity, and cost of work done. Payment specifications should be based on a measure of output or fixed price, and must include penalties for nonperformance. For example, the City retains the right to fine contractors for damages to park property that occur when jobs are being carried out or if work is incomplete. The Department currently fines contractors $250 per day if a mowing cycle is completed but the quality of the job remains unsatisfactory. Kansas City's contracts normally run for one year with options to renew for one additional year. The renewal option, accepted for 96 percent of 1993 contracts, provided a measure of contractors' program satisfaction levels.

Contract monitoring. Strict and consistent enforcement is critical to maintain the integrity of the process and the long-term success of the program. Superior enforcement begins with competent and close supervision. Initial relationships between contractors and inspectors are established at pre-bid meetings. Once contracts are signed, regularly scheduled meetings between contractors and inspectors are the norm. Inspectors document problems in writing as a matter of policy. In addition, photographic documentation is collected if deemed necessary, and inspectors are backed by cancellation clauses.

Although the Department has not had problems related to enforcement, staff have remained vigilant in regard to such procedures. Poor enforcement would result in deterioration of facility and program quality, and damage the agency's reputation. Poor enforcement also might result in lower bids submitted to the agency in future years by careless contractors who know they can get by without fulfilling contractual obligations. Poor enforcement would also increase future costs to bring facilities and programs back up to standard.

VII. Marketing to internal and/or external publics

Soliciting bids. If contracting is deemed appropriate, it becomes necessary to evaluate the contract option. It is essential to consider the issue of contractor availability. What is the number of potential qualified bidders? It is easy to overlook groups and businesses capable of completing the work, so the Department takes the solicitation process very seriously. Kansas City's began its initial bidder list by examining the *Yellow Pages* listings. However, the Department does not rely solely on the phone book to solicit bids, but instead aggressively advertises bids in newspapers for a minimum of five days under several listings. In addition, the Department contacts previous suppliers of related services, talks with other public agencies that contract for similar services, and meets with professional associations in order to produce the largest possible bidding pool. The larger the bidding pool, the lower the bids. Between twenty and twenty-five bidders were expected to compete for 1994 mowing contracts, of which ten to twelve would receive bids.

City staff also develop an annual notice to direct mail to contractors that includes date, time, and location of the City's Pre-Bid Conference and Bid Opening for maintenance services. The notice specifies what information must accompany bids and provides an agency contact for additional assistance and to answer questions. The Pre-Bid Conference and Bid Opening is designed to provide maximum advantage to the Department of Parks and Recreation. It generally lasts between one and two hours and takes place in the off-season which allows for maximum preparation and participation by City staff. This timing also ensures that contracts are awarded and secured prior to the start of the mowing season. A small room is chosen for the Pre-Bid Conference to deliberately give a crowded impression. The previous year's bid tabulation is laid out for visual inspection and a slide presentation is shown detailing quality expectations. Departmental mowing inspectors from the City's four maintenance districts run the Pre-Bid Conference, to give the inspectors an opportunity to establish their expertise and authority. In addition, this arrangement allows inspectors to develop a rapport with the bidders and take them on tours of potential mowing sites. Several criteria are used to select contractors including: past performance, level of expertise, suitability of equipment/facilities, possession of appropriate licenses and permits, and insurability. Appendix A (page 172) outlines the time line for Kansas City's bidding process.

VIII. Impact of Change on the Agency

The Department is especially sensitive to issues related to Department morale and employee training. With respect to morale, it is critical to separate the areas maintained on contracts from those maintained by in-house crews. Interaction between the two groups should be minimized. This separation is easy to achieve in large, geographically dispersed communities like Kansas City.

The Department has also developed a Career Enhancement Program. This type of program became both possible and necessary as many permanent employees shifted to more complex, nonroutine maintenance responsibilities. This Career Enhancement Program is tailored to the needs of individual employees. For example, in early 1994, four subject areas were available in the area of motor equipment: (1) hands-on automotive computer and trouble codes training; (2) hands-on exhaust emission equipment training and Missouri statutes mandating same; (3) all inclusive antilock braking systems (ABS) training; and (4) long-term auto and truck study programs related to repairs, specifications and management.

IX. Impact of Change on the Community

Overall, Kansas City citizens have a very positive impression of the Department of Parks and Recreation. The positive impression is due primarily to the Department's reliability, i.e., its ability to deliver what it promised in a timely manner. The contracting program allowed the Park Maintenance Division to meet its stated commitment to park mowing schedules. Most park land is on a seven-day to fourteen-day schedule. These commitments are maintained despite the budgetary limitations described earlier. One indication of the community's continued confidence in the Department is their support for new projects and initiatives. Recently, Kansas City voters approved a $50 million bond issue for the construction of a new City Zoo.

The Department's contracting program was also a successful vehicle for starting and supporting small businesses. Several companies formed specifically to bid for Park mowing contracts. Many of these companies are able to purchase capital equipment on the basis of these early revenue sources and moved on to other private sector contracts (e.g., office complexes, apartment complexes) as well as other governmental work.

X. Measurement of the Outcome

Contracts are evaluated on an annual basis by the Parks Division manager and the field inspectors. Four questions are asked by the personnel charged with conducting contract evaluations.

First, was the contract cost-effective or were there additional unexpected results? Appendix A (page 173) clearly demonstrates that the Kansas City Department of Parks and Recreation successfully decreased mowing and litter related maintenance costs on a cost per acre basis over the past eight years.

Second, do the contract specifications need to be revised?

Third, what was the impact on service levels for other work activities? Standards are now set in a variety of areas. For example, playgrounds are inspected on a monthly basis rather than "as often as possible" as was done in the past.

Fourth, does the scope of contract services need to be increased or decreased? This decision is based on the cumulative evidence provided by the first three questions.

Author's Suggested Readings and References

Bartling, M. L. (1979). *Contracting Recreation and Park Services.* Champaign, IL: Management Learning Laboratories.

Callihan, L. (1989, March). Contracting for services. *Grounds Maintenance.* Overland Park, KS: Intertec Publishing.

Clark, D. E. and Lampone, S. F. (July 1993). Contracting out park and recreation services. *Keeping You Current.* Rocky Hill, CT: National Recreation and Park Association.

Privatization and Contracting Out. Chicago, IL: Midwest Center for Labor Research.

Mundt, B., Olsen, R. T., and Steinberg, H. I. (1982). *Managing Public Resources.* New York, NY: Peat Marwick International.

Sociodemographic Characteristics—

Indianapolis

Indianapolis, Indiana

1990 Population:
> 731,327

Median Age:
> 31.6

Household Composition:
> 78.9% in families

Chapter 5

Private Management of Public Golf Courses

Indianapolis, Indiana

Leon Younger
Director of Parks and Recreation
Indianapolis Department of Parks and Recreation

I. The Situation

The Indianapolis Department of Parks and Recreation (Indy Parks) operated twelve municipal golf courses in 1992 but many concerns about golf operations were expressed by both the golfing public and city officials. A general lack of accountability in operations resulted in unacceptable maintenance levels and poor service for Indianapolis' municipal golfers.

Problematic accountability existed due to the fact that three groups of people were involved in servicing the public golf courses. Each entity functioned within a separate accountability chain.

First, *golf pros* were contracted to promote golf and teach lessons. The pros' budgets were based on 90 percent of cart rental fees, ten percent of green fees, and 100 percent of concessions and pro shop sales. Twelve pros controlled operations at the twelve City courses.

Second, golf course maintenance was assigned to 42 *city employees*, 30 of whom were union members. Because of high base salaries and overtime rates, the Department paid much more for course maintenance (as a percentage of green fees) than the industry average. Another problem related to the employee base was a lack of equipment needed to maintain the courses properly. A high percentage of revenues went into salaries. The City was unsuccessful in hiring and retaining a sufficient number of skilled and committed employees to be dedicated to improving the courses for the City's golfers. The majority of the employees lacked appreciation for golf.

Third, major equipment purchases and repairs were the responsibility of the City's *Central Equipment Maintenance Division* (CEMD). Most CEMD personnel were not golfers, and, therefore, lacked the commitment and dedication necessary to improve the City's golf courses. Complaints regarding poor service, length of time needed to service equipment, and the high cost associated with CEMD services were common.

In summary, the three-tiered golf operations system was ineffective and inefficient. When faced with a problem or complaint, a lot of between-group fingerpointing took place before action could be taken to solve problems. No one accepted responsibility to find solutions in part because there was little incentive built into this system to encourage reliable and responsive service.

II. Vision

Indy Parks officials envisioned a golf operation that was accountable to customers; including golfers, suppliers and the Department. Indy Parks further envisioned the golf courses operating in a competitive manner with both each other and the private marketplace, yet providing a range of opportunities for municipal golfers.

III. Objectives

Indy Parks developed three simple objectives to achieve their vision:

1. Reduce costs for maintenance and repairs.

2. Improve customer service.

3. Increase available funds for improvements.

IV. Management Paradigm Shift

The paradigm shift involved releasing golf course management from the City's bureaucracy and the restrictions regarding exclusively using City employees and maintenance services to a system that would allow golf course management to contract services.

V. Key Players

The review committee included two representatives of the Mayor's office, two representatives of the influential citizen group SELTIC (Service, Efficiency, and Lower Taxes for Indianapolis Commission), one member of the citizen Parks Board, the Indy Parks Golf Administrator, the Director of Indy Parks, and the Indy Parks Legal Counsel.

VI. Processes Undertaken to Accomplish Change

During the summer of 1992, the Review Committee spent several months developing the criteria upon which potential bidders for golf course management would be asked to develop proposals. A Request For Proposals (RFP), released with sample management contracts, addressed everything required to improve golf operations. Initially, all potential bidders were judged on their ability to teach golf and their ability to play golf in accordance with Professional Golfers' Association (PGA) standards.

The Review Committee identified as many measurable areas as possible to ensure a fair bidding process. These measurable areas would ensure that desired standards would be met by all successful bidders. These criteria fell into one of two categories.

The first category was price attributes and revenue projections. The Review Committee requested three-year revenue projections for green fees, golf cart rentals, concessions, driving ranges and pro shops. Price-related attributes accounted for 50 percent of the weight in the final decision.

The second set of criteria involved nonprice attributes. These also accounted for 50 percent of the weight in the final decision. The seven nonprice criteria utilized in developing and evaluating proposals are as follows:

Management skills were defined as the availability of effective management systems and methods appropriate to the successful management of the golf course. In addition, potential contractors needed to provide evidence that they had a sufficient number of competent personnel with appropriate management skills. Examples of general guidelines for the evaluation of proposals included:

(a) Is the management structure focused on meeting the contract requirements as outlined in the RFP?

(b) Is the organization's structure appropriate for this contract?

(c) How much daily contact will the pro have involving operations?

(d) What quality control measures for customer service are identified?

The second area, *existing track record,* referred to the potential contractor's prior record of completing work projects to the required standard, on time and within budget. Consideration of contractor employees was also made. This consideration related primarily to the pro's management group, but new professional contractors were also considered. The general guideline for this evaluation was: "Based on their existing track record, is the contractor likely to perform satisfactorily for the duration of the contract?"

Technical skills encompassed the competence of the personnel and the proposed contractor with particular regard to their skills and experience in comparable technical areas. Technical skills included pro shop operations, concession operations, course maintenance, operation experience, equipment maintenance experience, and driving range experience. Technical skills applied only to the proposed course personnel, other than the pro; management skills were not included in this category. General guidelines included:

(a) What technical skills are deemed necessary for this contract?

(b) Is the level of technical skill sufficient to achieve the quality required?

(c) Is there confidence in the proposed personnel?

(d) If skills are barely sufficient, can they be improved by cross-training within the contractor's organization?

Resources included the equipment available, the facilities, and golf course property which the contractor proposed to use. Subcontractors identified as being used for the contractual work were considered resources available to the contractor. Heavy reliance on subcontractual elements, however, requires good management skills to coordinate the work. General guidelines included:

(a) Does the contract propose the correct and sufficient amount of supplies and equipment to undertake the work?

(b) Is the proposed facility adequate enough to provide the required services?

(c) Are the proposed labor resources sufficient to cover the golf course area and the responsibilities described for it in the RFP? (Judgment and productivity levels should be avoided.)

(d) Are adequate financial resources proposed to operate the course?

Relevant experience referred to the potential contractor's previous experience in contract works of comparable scale and content. It specifically related to the person's or company's experience in managing golf courses. General guidelines included:

(a) Recent experience is much more valuable than historic experience.

(b) Has the contractor undertaken this type of work before?

(c) Can the contractor modify existing experience to this type of work?

(d) If applicable, is the contractor able to shift from existing management responsibilities to the required responsibilities as outlined in the RFP process?

Methodology referred to the procedures and methods the contractor proposed to use in order to achieve the specific end result. The contractor needed to demonstrate an understanding of the job and the best way to achieve the desired results. General guidelines included:

(a) Has the contractor proposed an appropriate methodology to accomplish this type of work?

(b) Does the submission focus on the needs of the contract?

(c) How are records and information to be assembled?

(d) How will regular reports to the golf administrator be undertaken?

(e) How will quality control be assured?

Quality of the proposal related to the question: Does the proposal meet the requirements of the RFP so that the evaluators can appropriately address the points they need to make a sound decision? General guidelines included:

(a) No specific pieces of information outlined in the RFP request can be omitted from any proposal.

(b) Capital improvement priorities must be outlined.

Potential contractors were permitted to bid on management contracts for one or all of the twelve City golf courses. Twenty-seven proposals from eighteen different bidders were received during the months of August and September 1992. Five of the courses received only one bid, whereas as many as six contractors bid on two of the courses. Proposals were individually reviewed, weighed and scored by an eight member evaluation team that included a team leader, the Director of Parks and Recreation and six expert judges. Following the individual rating process, proposals were then ranked in order of point scores and priority. Ranges for percentages of revenue were negotiated on two grounds—first, the percentage of gross revenue for green fees, carts, concessions, and driving range (8 percent to 24 percent), and second, the percentage of gross receipts from the pro shop (3 percent to 10 percent).

Each proposal was also graded relative to the seven nonprice attributes using a four-point scale where: 0 = entirely inadequate, 1 = below average (barely adequate and would need improvement if selected), 2 = average (minor deficiencies not likely to adversely affect operations), 3 = good (all requirements are fully covered), and 4 = excellent (all requirements met to an outstanding degree). The evaluation team eliminated all proposals that rated a zero on any of the seven criteria from further consideration. A sample of Indy Parks' Golf Course Proposal Evaluation Sheet is shown in Appendix B (page 175).

Reviewers met with each management company or individual pro to discuss and critique their proposals and examine their operational plans during the months of September, October and November 1992. The specifications included cleanliness standards, maintenance standards, and customer service operations. During the meetings bidders were given the opportunity to articulate in-depth how they would manage a golf course. The evaluation team then made recommendations for awarding bids based on composite scores generated based on price-related and nonprice-related criteria.

The Parks Board approved the management contracts after receiving recommendations from the evaluation team. One pro who was not retained protested that the process was unfair. Overall, the Department retained six pros and gained six new pros. By providing a good balance of new and old, Indy Parks staff believed their efforts to be in the best interest of the community's golfers. This process outline resulted in the creation of an efficient, entrepreneurial system. Successful bidders committed to the City for four-year periods by signing a detailed 29-page Golf Professional Agreement with Indy Parks.

VII. Marketing to Internal and/or External Publics

Concurrent with the release of RFPs in early August, Indy Parks staff announced the Department's intentions to the PGA, and communicated Departmental expectations to the pros. Each pro employed by the City was required to submit a proposal if he desired to keep his job as a pro. The PGA endorsed the plan.

Following PGA approval, Department administrators announced the plan to the union, and explained that under the new system, they would no longer be City employees, but could be hired by the pro or be placed somewhere else in City government. Many of the City employees were in fact reemployed by the golf pros as parts of their new organizations. Local media coverage carried the message to the public.

VIII. Impact of Change on the Agency

By contracting the management of the golf courses to pros, the Department ensured that all operational decisions would be made by someone who is dedicated to the golfer. Indy Parks also cleared the way for individual pros to hire staff as equally committed as they are to servicing the City's golfers. It is expected that this change in operating policy will result in a higher level of job satisfaction for the City's golf employees.

By introducing competition into the system, Indy Parks staff are confident that a higher level of service can be attained, even as the courses become more cost efficient. This allows golf operations to increase productivity with the money available.

The unionized work force faced a salary cutback, if they decided to stay with the golf operations.

The Central Equipment Maintenance Division (CEMD) no longer services golf equipment for Indy Parks.

Indy Parks identified two sources of opportunity dollars that will return to support improvements of golf courses:

1. $1.0 million from each pro, and

2. Season pass income ($0.5 million) that will fund the golf course administration budget, capital equipment replacement program, and emergency capital program for golf course repair.

The city issued revenue bonds that will allow Indy Parks to make improvements. This policy will allow Indy Parks to double back revenue from golf into the courses. A key component involved a $150,000 line of credit with the bank for each course so the contractors would not put themselves in a cash flow crunch.

To date, all pro shops have experienced cosmetic improvements; weekday fees are slightly higher; and season pass holders (except patrons who are senior citizens) now pay a $1 surcharge.

IX. Impact of Change on the Community

By privatizing management of the golf courses, Indy Parks laid the framework for their golf operations to function in a competitive market. The pros now have the opportunity, and obligation to maintain a high level of service and quality at their course(s).

At last a system of accountability for golf operations is in place. Indy Parks anticipates that this new management system will result in intensification of service levels, improvement of courses, and, as a result will increase the patronage of public courses.

Surveys received by the Department have indicated that the golfing public is extremely pleased with the improvements made to each course. Respondents have encouraged the Department to continue with its contracting policy.

X. Measurement of the Outcome

Each pro's proposal specified a standard of excellence for the course that focused on maintenance, capital improvements, and customer service. Indy Parks will measure each course against set standards by employing a mystery shopper program. The mystery shopper program will be implemented by retired executives of Indy Parks who will play and evaluate the courses and their services. The Director and Golf Administrator of Indy Parks will visit the courses as well. With this program, Indy Parks intends to give the pros constant and consistent feedback about their progress. A third program is a direct feedback mechanism from golfers to the Department that is titled "How did we score?"

Author's Suggested Readings and References

Golf Professional Agreement. (1992). Available from the City of Indianapolis Department of Parks and Recreation.

Sociodemographic Characteristics—

Baltimore, Maryland

1990 Population:
736,014
Median Age:
32.5
Household Composition:
76.1% in families

Chapter 6

Baltimore Municipal Golf Corporation (BMGC): Not-For-Profit Golf Course Management[2]

Baltimore, Maryland

Lynnie Cook
Executive Director
Baltimore Municipal Golf Corporation

I. The Situation

A recent article in *Golf World* noted that

> "in most municipalities, public golf courses resemble Russian markets. Long lines and inferior product cause many muny (municipal) golfers to conclude that their green fees are lost somewhere in a whirlwind of bureaucratic inefficiency. Usually they're right. If a municipal course makes money, the profits end up funding things like city workers' softball uniforms instead of neglected bunkers" (Lee, 1993, p. 16).

Although once home to some top municipal courses, Baltimore faced similar problems ten years ago. During the late 1970s and early 1980s, the City of Baltimore lost a half million dollars per year operating its five municipal golf courses. The lack of profitability resulted in deteriorating course and clubhouse conditions, declining patronage, and poor employee morale.

The list of dissatisfied clients was not limited to local golfers. The Professional Golfers' Association (PGA) and Ladies Professional Golf Association (LPGA) relocated two tour events, traditionally held on Baltimore City courses, to other cities. The final blow came when *Golf Digest* magazine removed Baltimore's Pine Ridge Golf Course from its Top 100 listing of courses. The principal causes of this downward spiral were grouped into four areas: contracts, employees, funding, and politics.

Contracts. The City's golf professionals received 100 percent of the revenue from the pro shop, food service, and driving range. They also

---

[2] Winner of the Reily Award for the outstanding change model presented at the 1993 Models of Change Conference.

received 80 percent of the revenue from golf cart rentals. Haphazard accounting procedures resulted in the lack of an audit trail.

Employees. Wages represented 85 percent of the City's golf operating budget compared to the golf industry standard of approximately 57 percent of costs. The major problem involved the fact that the City employed too many full-time workers (about 120) and never utilized workers at any of its courses. Although the five municipal courses remained open year-round, approximately 75 percent of all rounds were played in the eight-month period beginning in late March and ending in early December. Demand was simply not adequate enough to support such a large full-time staff year-round.

In addition, the benefits package grew to between 40 percent and 50 percent of employee wages. Leave and overtime policies were also excessive compared with industry standards. Employees received compensation time, vacation time, and mental health days in addition to over fifteen holidays per year recognized by the Department.

Equipment repairs, conducted by the off-site, central maintenance department, were slow, unreliable and expensive. Problems often occurred because equipment repair priorities established by the central office would prioritize a lawn mower designed for manicuring golf course greens below a mower designed for mowing highway medians since the median mower arrived for repairs first. This created problems for the golf courses since greens must be trimmed on a daily basis, but highway medians are generally cut about two or three times per year.

Funding. The budget for materials and supplies was reduced to only two percent of the entire operating budget, well below the golf industry's average. The reduction in supplies was how the City dealt with maintaining wage, staff and benefit levels. As a result, the capital improvements budget was eliminated for most of the early 1980s.

Politics. Fee schedules were artificially low. Prior to the management changes, it was less expensive to play eighteen holes at one of the courses than it was to buy lunch at a McDonald's restaurant. Excessive courtesy play was also a problem. Politicians, sports figures, and friends of employees routinely played for free. In addition, golf pros received 100 percent of pro shop revenues, and granted perks such as free rounds of golf for major purchases like a new set of clubs.

Crucial operating decisions required immediate action, but were often held up by multiple park board and city council meetings. The slow nature of the decision-making process was not a deliberate attempt to harm golf operations. Annual budgets for course maintenance which were set months in advance proved difficult to adjust even under abnormal circumstances. For example, turfgrass diseases flourish during particularly hot, wet summers, but emergency requests for supplies to combat these diseases still had to go through the Parks Department and Purchasing Department to meet the City's standards for financial accountability. Additional problems arose from many politically motivated management decisions, some of which proved detrimental to the long-range interest of the majority of municipal golfers, and interest groups and individuals close to City Council members held disproportionate influence concerning pricing policies.

II. Vision

To create "country club" conditions at affordable prices while maintaining the cash flow to ensure long-term growth and improvement of the facilities.

III. Objectives

Parks Department Staff developed four objectives, consistent with the vision of the change model:

1. To ensure financial viability of the City's courses. Operations were expected to be self-sufficient. Fiscal responsibility for golf operations was transferred to the new management team.

2. To increase the rounds of golf played on an annual basis to attain levels which would allow long-term success within five years.

3. To improve course and clubhouse conditions by annual investment of sufficient funds to implement meaningful capital improvement plans.

4. To create an ongoing junior golf program for inner-city youth who, as a group, play very little golf.

IV. Management Paradigm Shift

To create an organization free of bureaucratic red-tape and to implement a system based upon sound business principles. This action would allow management to concentrate on, and quickly address the needs of the golfing public.

V. Key Players

In 1984, then Mayor William Donald Schafer formed a Mayoral Committee chaired by Bernie Trueschler, President and CEO of Baltimore Gas and Electric Company, to review and analyze current golf operations and make appropriate recommendations. The nine-member committee consisted of: the Director of Parks and Recreation (Baltimore City), the Director of Golf Course Maintenance (Baltimore City), and seven prominent business leaders and executives. Although the Mayor was not a member of the committee officially, he was the one who recognized the need to make bold changes in the management of the City's golf facilities.

VI. Processes Undertaken to Accomplish Change

After reviewing many management alternatives, the Committee presented four options to the Mayor in late 1984. Those options were:

A. *Maintain the current management under the Department of Parks and Recreation.* The City would retain power, and have greater control over the courses than under any of the other three proposed scenarios. Considerable public concern developed that if the courses were not managed by the City, fees would become too expensive for the average player. However, the negative consequences of maintaining the status quo, relating to contracts, employees, funding and politics, as outlined earlier in this chapter, still needed to be overcome.

B. *Create a city-run golf course authority.* The three advantages projected for this option were:

(1) it would maintain the City's control over golf operations;

(2) capital could be raised through the promotion of municipal bond issues; and

(3) the City would maintain potential revenues within the purview of the authority.

The major disadvantage was that the authority would be taxed by the same employee and political problems that existed under the current system.

C. *Lease the five municipal courses as a package to a private contractor through competitive bidding.* The two major advantages anticipated from this option were:

(1) Private golf contractors have proven experience with multigolf course management. Several private golf management firms operated in the United States in the mid-1980s.

(2) The lease was expected to provide the City with positive income in contrast to the annual losses being incurred.

However, several disadvantages were also identified.

First, a portion of the profits would leave the state since no private golf course management firms were based in Maryland. This scenario was politically unacceptable because Mayor Schafer was a proponent of the "do it with Baltimore people" philosophy.

Second, private management firms are subject to income taxes which would reduce operating profits, and, consequently, the amount of money that could be used for course improvements. For every $1 million dollars in net income, $300,000 in taxes would accrue at a corporate tax rate of 30 percent.

Third, there was widespread concern that personal and private interest would take precedent over the public's interest. This could result in unacceptably high prices and limited course access.

D. *Create a not-for-profit management corporation.* Several potential benefits were outlined.

First, by law, all of the profits would be returned to support the golf courses. It creates a system whereby golfers support other golfers because revenue would not be diverted to the general fund. In addition, the corporation would be tax-exempt.

Second, this option effectively removes politics from business decisions. Day-to-day management decisions would be streamlined because they would be separate from the normal municipal bureaucratic processes.

Third, payroll problems would be reduced since the not-for-profit corporations operate separately from the existing City labor unions.

Finally, unlike Option C, this option would keep almost all revenues within the municipality because the corporation would be run by and for Baltimoreans.

Both the Parks Department and local press opposed the private not-for-profit option. The Parks Department disagreed with this direction because it threatened existing employees, and the press was skeptical primarily because a private, not-for-profit golf operation had never been attempted. The consensus of the media was that it was unrealistic to expect a new, inexperienced management team to turn the mismanaged golf system around without a dramatic increase in prices. Nevertheless, the Mayor, confident that Baltimore had the talent to manage the five courses if they were removed from politician's control, opted to create the nation's first not-for-profit golf management company. It was worth taking note of the willingness of the Mayor and other senior City leaders to risk their political futures since the expected payoffs involving the changes in course management would accrue, if at all, on a long-term basis. The Mayor directed the City to provide the newly formed Company, Baltimore Municipal Golf Corporation (BMGC), with a $125,000 bridge loan to cover payroll expenses during the first month and to provide a $350,000 line of credit for the purchase of equipment. The new corporation qualified as a tax-exempt 501(C)3 corporation under Internal Revenue Service guidelines without problems.

VII. Marketing to Internal and/or External Publics

Internal. Once the decision was made to pursue the not-for-profit alternative, existing employees had the opportunity to join the new Company or remain with the City of Baltimore. If they joined the new Company, they would be subject to all of the Company's guidelines and regulations. The exception to this offer was the wage scale. Under the agreement, former city employees would maintain their existing city wage until the new Company's wage scale caught up with theirs. Only three of the approximately 120 employees assigned to golf courses before the change in management elected to stay with BMGC; the remaining employees transferred to other city departments. This was not surprising given the negative press regarding the private not-for-profit alternative, the loss of some union benefits, and the indefinite, de facto pay freeze until BMGC's wages surpassed the existing city scale. BMGC initiated new employees into their culture and procedures as part of the normal learning curve. BMGC's full-time employees currently receive two to four weeks of annual vacation leave and two paid holidays, a 401K retirement plan, participation in the BMGC bonus plan, full health coverage, and life insurance benefits, plus sick leave.

External. Many public meetings, designed to convey information on the direction of the new Company, to answer questions, and to dispel rumors, were held at various locations including each of the five municipal courses. BMGC's Board of Directors, an all volunteer body, ran the meetings and provided information. Those who attended the meetings included various independent golf organizations, seniors, private citizens, the media and existing members of the course clubs (e.g., Men's, Women's and Seniors'). Their questions focused on projected rates and improvements, outings restrictions, and what, if any, changes the new corporation would propose about existing privileges. Although BMGC attempted to address proactively the many questions and concerns plaguing the project by sponsoring the public meetings, the general tenor of the proceedings reflected distrust and fear fueled largely by the numerous rumors surrounding the project. The meetings did little to dispel these fears. These concerns and fears began to abate, however, when golfers' actual experiences and course performance suggested that the new policies actually worked quite well.

VIII. Impact of Change on the Agency

Several impacts of the change on the agency were apparent. First, an immediate half-million dollar savings for the Department of Recreation and Parks accrued as jurisdiction for the money-losing courses transferred to BMGC. Much of this savings was attributable to the accounting shift, although additional savings resulted from reduced city payroll and retirements. Second, the value of the City's golf assets improved since money was once again being returned to capital improvements. National recognition was forthcoming from the United States Golf Association (USGA), National Golf Foundation (NGF) and *Golf World* magazine. The value of the City's golf course assets could be communicated regularly by BMGC, which produces regular financial statements—a benefit that both golfers and nongolfing taxpayers lacked when the courses were under City management.

Politicians who supported the proposed change received public praise in the print media for taking this creative step toward improving the courses. Specifically, the decision to form BMGC was described as a smart and courageous decision with positive long-term consequences that outweighed the short-term risk. Members of the local press admitted they made a mistake in their prejudgment of this innovative management approach. One prominent Baltimore sports columnist issued a public, written apology for his opposition to this change process.

Finally, other Department programs benefited from the financial success of BMGC. The original contract mandated no payments to the City. However, when it became apparent that BMGC would have a positive balance sheet, city politicians and Corporate officials agreed that the Company would establish a trust fund for city youth. The City now receives a fixed $225,000 annual payment to the trust from BMGC. To date, this fund has been used to support programming for a diverse range of youth activities including basketball, football, track, chess, and marching bands. The money is also used to send championship caliber local teams to regional and national events. Youth golf programs are funded by BMGC directly and, therefore, are not part of the trust.

IX. Impact of Change on the Community

Three positive impacts of the change were immediately apparent to Baltimore's municipal course golfers.

First, the courses play faster. Over the past few years BMGC decreased the average playing time from five and one-half hours to four and one-quarter hours through more money which was allocated for course marshals and other support staff.

Second, the paying public sees their money at work improving the courses. In the ten years since BMGC assumed responsibility for golf operations, wages dropped from 85 percent to 56 percent of the budget. Consequently, materials, supplies, and other components of the capital improvements budget rose from two percent to 34 percent of the total operating budget.

Third, contrary to initial predictions by many Baltimoreans, the five municipal courses have the lowest fee schedule in the mid-Atlantic states. Greens fees range from $8 to $11.50 per round. Had rates risen at the rate of inflation since 1986, 1993 greens fees would be $13.50 per round at the City's top course.

The number of full-time employees dropped from approximately 120 to 60 at the five courses. This drop in employees came primarily at the expense of the union positions within the Parks Department's maintenance division. However, by decreasing the number of full-time positions and increasing the operations budget, the Company could employ more seniors and young adults. The junior golf program (see Vision #4) targeted primarily inner city youth. Rather than run trespassing youth off of the courses in their neighborhoods, as had been past City practice, BMGC works to get them involved in the game. This program not only provides constructive activity for the youth and build future markets for municipal courses, but it also decreases vandalism since a higher percentage of the City's youth developed an interest in the courses.

X. Measurement of the Outcome

Numerous tangible accomplishments can be documented in the ten year history of BMGC, which easily surpassed any expectations that the City had regarding the success of the corporation. Total rounds of golf at the five municipal courses rose from 195,000 rounds in 1984 to more than 360,000 rounds annually by 1993. Over $2.6 million in capital improvements were invested into the five courses from 1985 to 1993. Most of these improvements were made following BMGC's repayment of the $125,000 bridge loan that the Mayor supplied in 1984. The loan was repaid after just two years—three full years ahead of schedule. In 1987, *Golf Digest* magazine placed Pine Ridge Golf Course back onto its list of Top 100 Courses. Although Pine Ridge no longer holds this distinction in deference to the new courses that are being developed across the United States, it along with its sister course, Mt. Pleasant, is rated as one of the Top Ten public courses in the three state area surrounding Baltimore (Maryland, Delaware, and Virginia). It should also be noted that BMGC's maintenance and operations (clubhouse) budgets are comparable to area country clubs. These standards are maintained even though Baltimoreans play on municipal courses which boast the lowest fees in the mid-Atlantic states.

Although financial stability and facility improvement are dramatic, the positive attitude of the BMGC staff and appreciation of the public are the real benchmarks of BMGC's success. The Company is developing plans to build a sixth golf course without the use of public funds. The new course plans include a three-hole facility which will be accessible to residents with physical handicaps and a nature center that will take advantage of the natural setting surrounding the proposed course. BMGC is currently exploring the possibilities of integrating programs with school science classes—an arrangement, that if brought to fruition, would represent yet another innovative idea developed to provide long-term benefits to the city.

Author's Suggested Readings and References

Lee, A. S. (1993, March 5). Baltimore's better idea. *Golf World, 46*(24), pp. 16-20.

Section Two:
Societal and Political Change Models

This section includes six cases related to social and political change and some organized recreation agencies' efforts to address those changes. The first four cases in this section address social change; the latter two address political change.

The first case describes Lake Farmpark of Lake County, Ohio—an innovative park constructed to educate Lake County's primarily suburban population and area visitors about the wonders and complexities of modern agriculture and how that industry interacts with surrounding urban and suburban environments.

The next case describes the West Des Moines' Read-to-Me program which addresses the realities faced by many children and senior citizens who often have little opportunity to interact with each other as compared to interactive opportunities available to earlier generations. Declines in the percentage of extended family households and the increased mobility of society represent only two of the societal changes addressed by the Read-to-Me program.

Third, the Indiana Sports Corporation (ISC) represents an innovative agency developed to diversify the central Indiana economy which can no longer depend on manufacturing-based industries to the extent it did in the past. The programs and facilities developed based on ISC initiatives have not only diversified the state's economy, but have also facilitated programs and events that have a positive impact on the general quality of life for all residents and improved the health and wellness of many individuals.

The ISC's ProKids program, the fourth societal case, represents an effort targeted specifically to a subgroup within Indiana's broader population—its youth. ISC facilitates youth programming efforts among Indianapolis' diverse community of professional athletic teams.

The fifth and sixth cases discuss political change.

Waco Texas' Leisure Services Department undertook a complete restructuring program which changed the agency's orientation from that of a traditional, passive (i.e., take it or leave it) direct provider of recreation services to a facilitator of recreation, tourism programs and events. In doing so, Waco Leisure Services forged ongoing cooperative relationships with the local convention and visitors bureau and with several cultural and leisure service organizations.

The final case in this section describes the Illinois' Arlington Heights Park District. The District recognized that it was underutilizing tremendous internal staff resources with its traditional top down management system. Its new philosophy allowed the delegation of authority, related to diverse issues such as equipment purchases to customer service, to extend to all employees in the system. This attempt at decentralization resulted in higher levels of satisfaction among park and recreation participants and better morale among District staff.

Sociodemographic Characteristics—

Lake County

Lake County, Ohio

1990 Population:

215,499

Median Age:

34.2

Household Composition:

86.6% families

Chapter 7

Lake Farmpark:
An Open-Air Science and Cultural Center

Lake County, Ohio

Darwin Kelsey
Farmpark Administrator
Lake Metroparks

I. The Situation

Lake County is located on the south shore of Lake Erie, just east of Cleveland, Ohio. Population growth intensified after World War II, and effectively changed the character of the county from a countryside dominated by dairy farms, orchards and nurseries to a predominantly suburban community. Lake Metroparks operates as a special district with its own taxation powers, separate from county government. A three-member authoritative Board of Commissioners who are appointed by an elected probate judge manage the district.

Public surveys of Lake County residents conducted in 1985-86 identified widespread support for Lake Metroparks with a strong interest in improvement and expansion of the park system. Based partially on the survey results, the Board of Commissioners authorized expansion efforts. In the fall of 1986, Lake County voters passed a 1.9 mill tax levy which, at the time, was the highest levy in the history of the state. The levy facilitated land acquisition, trail and facility improvements in nature parks, introduction of recreation programming to the park system, and development of special facilities (e.g., beach and marina areas, winter sports facilities, and an historical-agricultural park).

In 1987 Commissioners initiated radical changes in park administration and operation including: the removal of the existing Executive Director, the recruitment of a new Executive Director from outside the park system, the national recruitment of support staff, and an authorization of staff growth totaling nearly 400 percent over three years. The property destined to house the Farmpark was purchased in 1987. Formerly an Arabian horse farm, the Farmpark consisted of four existing barns and an indoor arena.

II. Vision

The vision that became Lake Farmpark evolved over a period of several years. Planning for the new park began in 1988, even though the administrator was not hired until 1989. Early concepts for the development of an agricultural park to preserve the region's farming and nursery heritage were based primarily on historical village and living historical farms projects which became popular in the last several decades. However, an attempt to incorporate a Kentucky Horse Park[3] type program tended to compromise these historical village and farm concepts. Moreover, early planning failed to take into account the multimillion dollar capital requirements necessary when developing high quality living history sites. Most well-known sites have more than twenty buildings. Restoration and construction costs average over $500,000 per building. Another limitation involved the recent proliferation of historic villages. Over 200 such sites now operate in the United States and Canada. Several are within convenient driving distance of Lake County including Century Village and Hale Farm in north central Ohio, and nationally significant parks such as Dearborn, Michigan's, Greenfield Village. High capital costs and the presence of these nearby competitors suggested that construction of a living history site was a restrictive and limited option for the Lake Metropark system.

Early conceptualizations of Lake Farmpark also failed to consider emerging ideas to address the environmental illiteracy of modern urbanites and suburbanites. The number of farmers in the U.S. has fallen from more than 90 percent of the population in 1800 to less than three percent in the 1990s. Few Americans understand modern agricultural science or how farming evolved in the past century. In fact, many people are so divorced from food production processes that visitors at working and historical farms sometimes mistake calves for sheep, have little notion of where butter or hamburger comes from, or understand that most pickles originate as cucumbers. A 1991 Gallup survey revealed that 49 percent of all Americans could not identify the main ingredient in white bread.

The vision for Lake Farmpark proposed in 1989 by the park's new administrator was:

1. To create a new kind of place specifically designed to address modern urban Americans' disconnection from nature and agriculture;

2. To go beyond the objectives and capabilities of existing historical villages and living historical farms;

---

[3] A large state-operated theme park in Kentucky's thoroughbred country. Its programming focuses on horses and their relationship to society.

3. To borrow ideas and techniques from open-air museums, living history farms, agricultural and natural history museums, European farmparks, children's museums and science centers, zoos and wildlife parks, botanical and horticultural gardens by adapting and recombining them in new ways; and,

4. To create a new paradigm—farmpark.

In summary, the goal of Lake Farmpark was to be a mission—a market-driven park that would achieve far-reaching public interest (i.e., locally, regionally and nationally), prominent interest among educators, significant potential for financial support from foundations and corporations, and a notable degree of self-generated revenue.

III. Objectives

Lake Metroparks developed five objectives to guide the creation of the Farmpark:

1. To establish a historical-cultural-science park focused on farming, agriculture and country life for the use and enjoyment of Lake County residents.

2. To create a unique, quality park that attracts broad regional attendance among both local residents and tourists.

3. To create a unique, quality park that attracts broad regional and national financial support from foundations and corporations.

4. To develop awareness among the Lake Metropark's staff of the distinct differences between the capital needs, operating procedures and programming objectives of this farmpark-type facility as opposed to traditional nature parks and recreational programs with which staff are familiar.

5. To develop awareness and acceptance among Lake County residents for the need to charge admission fees for the park, which, though new, was part of a system which had never charged general admission fees, and part of the same system which had just received a major increase in tax support to improve and expand the park system. Seventy-five percent self-sufficiency after five years of operation was projected—an objective that would place the Farmpark within the top end of the efficiency range of similar operations.

IV. Management Paradigm Shift

No previous park in the Lake County system received capital improvements on a scale which allowed extensive development of building and grounds, museum and science center quality exhibits, intensive year-round educational programming, extensive year-round daily programs for the general public and an expanded gift shop and food service operation. Nor had any park in the system ever charged general admission fees normally associated with this type of operation. Four challenges emerged.

The first was to create acceptance among long-time park employees still committed to a relatively strict nature park paradigm. These employees needed to be convinced that a Farmpark could have a legitimate ecological and environmental message. The agency's previous programming emphasized nature-based parks featuring hiking trails, interpretive centers and picnic areas. These parks were all designed and programmed to enable participants to interact with or in a natural rather than cultivated environment.

A second challenge was to convince a group of park employees committed to the classic park and recreation paradigm that open-air museum and science center type exhibits, demonstrations and educational programs could be both popular and fun. Like many park and recreation agencies' staff, Lake Metroparks' are a diverse group of professionals with distinctive training, perspectives, and values. Hence, due to the occasionally divergent priorities of the nature staff and recreation staff, Farmpark staff added new priorities which were seen as competition for agency resources.

A third challenge was to convince park administrators of the need to construct buildings, acquire equipment, animals, specialized staff and other resources atypical to the Metroparks system. This challenge was more acute at middle-management levels than at upper-management levels since the Farmpark represented a major project that could take funds from existing parks and programs operated by middle-level management personnel.

Finally, Farmpark administration endeavored to create a specialized operational staff able to handle not only tasks unique to the Farmpark (e.g., agricultural exhibits, farm animal care), but tasks handled elsewhere by the park system from central offices (e.g., maintenance, volunteer administration). This decentralized approach was envisioned to minimize inefficiency and the bureaucracy that was characteristic of many centralized operating systems.

V. Key Players

The change process began in the mid-1980s with the three park commissioners who authorized major changes in the park system. The consensus of these officials was that the Metropark system, though solid, was not reaching its full potential. The new Lake Metroparks' Executive Director, hired after a nationwide search in 1988, supported the change process, as did the new Division Head of Special Facilities and Recreation who introduced recreational programs and events to the Metroparks system. The Farmpark Administrator, hired in 1989, was given broad autonomy and support to conceptualize and implement the concept with Farmpark department heads and programmers. The coalition of key players remained functional in the past few years even though most of the individuals the Farmpark Administrator answers to have changed.

VI. Processes Undertaken to Accomplish Change

Initially, Metropark staff worked to create a mission statement and general master plan for the first ten years of development. Upon completion of this initial plan, staff concentrated on the establishment of short-term projects to be accomplished over one, two and three years (e.g., building construction; animal and equipment acquisition; exhibit design, fabrication and installation; development of school programs).

A diverse group of park staff was recruited and/or hired over a period of eighteen months including: the Division Head for Special Facilities and Recreation, the Farmpark Administrator, Farmpark department heads, programmers, and operational staff consisting of approximately 30 full-time staff, twenty part-time staff, and over 275 volunteers. Individual Metroparks/Farmpark teams evolved to complete designated projects as short-term, one-year, two-year, and three-year goals and objectives. Employees also developed an operational plan, with all associated policies and procedures, based in part on existing Metroparks policies and procedures, and in part, on the unique mission/circumstances of Farmpark.

VII. Marketing to Internal and/or External Publics

Some internal opposition, generally based on the diversion of funds from traditional nature-based programming, surfaced against the Farmpark project. Continuous dialogue between the Executive Director and park commissioners relating Farmpark's mission, project authorization, and budget control kept the opposition at a minimal level. Most staff supported the concept after they learned more about the project. In this sense, continuous dialogue between the Executive Director, the Division Head of Special Facilities and Recreation, the Farmpark Administrator, and other Lake Metroparks staff to explain and justify Farmpark concepts, projects, budgets and requests for support was vital.

External opposition was also minimal. Some local residents became used to a sleepy park system and preferred that relative lack of activity. Others opposed spending tax dollars on the Metropark system, in general, although these protesters were strongly out-voted in the 1986 bond election. External communication consisted of constant, positive presentations by staff members. Regular meetings, tours, and discussions with local and regional newspapers, as well as radio and television representatives, were utilized primarily to develop public awareness and interest in Farmpark's emerging programs, develop a public comfort level about the expenditure of tax funds. The Farmpark administrators scheduled media events every few weeks as the Farmpark took shape and began operations. Tangible events, such as the completion of new buildings and the arrival of new animals or equipment, provided the topical themes for these events. Specialized program announcements, brochures, and mailings were sent to all school administrators and teachers within 35 miles of the Farmpark to develop awareness about the park, its mission, and its educational programs.

VIII. Impact of Change on the Agency

Farmpark established precedents and a psychology for innovative programming beyond traditional nature park and recreation program paradigms. It helped create an agency-wide sense of possibility and desirability to achieve national quality programs.

The Farmpark project created a base of experience for managing large scale rapid growth which could then be applied to subsequent and future projects: how to select and work with outside designers and/or contractors; how to create and modify internal administrative procedures; and, how to establish standards of achievable quality and quantity for the resources available.

During the initial stages of development, Farmpark expenditures accounted for approximately twenty percent of all agency operational resources. This caused feelings of envy and resentment among the other Metroparks' divisions and departments over the amount of resources diverted to this new program area. These reactions, however, were largely dispelled as major agency resources eventually focused on launching other large-scale projects for the Metroparks system.

Farmpark's development demonstrated that even large scale projects can be launched successfully by focusing intensively upon the agency's overall resources for a specific project over a period of one or two years. Subsequently, Lake Metroparks opened a new lake front park and a new community park in 1992, and, in 1993, acquired a major golf facility.

Finally, the Farmpark project established precedents which made certain types of operational improvements easier for other departments: decentralization of computer hardware and software for desktop publishing; use of contracted professionals for exhibit design and fabrication; and establishing a climate to charge user fees.

IX. Impact of Change on the Community

Farmpark gave Lake Metroparks a high-profile park with a successful image early in the park system's ten-year levy period, thereby establishing public credibility, and a sense that tax dollars were being used wisely.

Farmpark's programs achieved popular acceptance by local and regional users quickly and produced steady attendance that rose to total over 160,000 visitors per year. It also became a source of community pride due to positive national recognition from park, museum, and educational professionals.

Acknowledged as the County's key tourist attraction, Farmpark outdistanced all other county attractions in the number of motor coach tours booked during 1992 and 1993. Thirty-six tours visited Farmpark in 1992 and 137 tours were scheduled for 1993. Most motor tours originate from other areas of Ohio, and the states of Pennsylvania, Michigan, New York, and the province of Ontario. Farmpark became an important regional educational resource: in its third year of operation, it attracted 36,000 students in 885 groups from fifteen counties.

X. Measurement of the Outcome

Farmpark's progress was measured in three ways. First, Lake Farmpark exists: it didn't in 1989, it did in 1990, and attendance grew rapidly:

Year	1990	1991	1992
Educational attendance	20,000	32,000	36,000
Total attendance	89,000	117,000	160,000

Second, operational self-support is increasing in both relative and absolute dollars:

Year	1990	1991	1992
Total Expenses	$1,710,000	$1,590,000	$1,660,000
Percent Self-Sufficiency	11%	20%	37%

Third, professional evaluation and recognition proved positive. Farmpark was featured in three professional publications: *Ohio Schools, Midwest Open Air Museum Magazine,* and *Museum News.* In addition, Farmpark received six professional awards to date:

- National Association of County Parks and Recreation Officials (NACPRO) Class I Award of Excellence—1991;
- Ohio Parks and Recreation Association (OPRA) New Program Award–Special Event—1991;
- OPRA Student Program Development Award—1991;
- OPRA Performing/Creative Arts Program Award—1992;
- Northern Ohio Live Education Award of Achievement—1991; and
- The Lake County Soil and Water Conservation District Operator of the Year—1991.

Author's Suggested Readings and References

Kelsey, D. P. (1991). Lake Farmpark: First of a new breed of open-air museums. *Midwest Open-Air Museums, 12*(1), pp. 12-16.

Kelsey, D. P. (1992). Mayfield fifth graders go down on the farm. *Ohio Schools, 69*(9), pp. 20-22.

Kelsey, D. P. (1993). The farmpark paradigm. *Museum News, 72*(4), pp. 50-53, 66.

Sociodemographic Characteristics—

West Des Moines, Iowa

1990 Population:
31,702

Median Age:
33.2

Household Composition:
79.3% in families

West Des Moines

Chapter 8

Intergenerational Read-To-Me Program

West Des Moines, Iowa

Christine Larson
Assistant Director
West Des Moines Department of Parks and Recreation

I. The Situation

Our nation's demographic characteristics evolved as the United States shifted from a country populated by families and young children to a country with a growing proportion of older persons. Extended intergenerational families who shared common living quarters were common earlier in this century, but now are relatively rare. In addition, society became so mobile that grandparents and grandchildren often do not live in the same city or state anymore. Therefore, opportunities for grandparent-grandchildren interaction and bonding may not be available.

Many sociologists and family studies specialists suggest that there is a need to link the young and old in common experiences. For example, in 1991 the Toronto Bureau of Municipal Research found that intergenerational programming develops an understanding between age groups which is critical in an aging society. The last White House Conference on Aging, titled "Linking Generations for the Caring Society," outlined the benefits of intergenerational experiences. These benefits include: creation of a sense of worth for people of all ages; more positive community feelings; improved educational achievement of youth; preservation of skills, experiences and values of older citizens; an increased sense of caring by and for youth; improved emotional and mental health of the aged; increased levels of understanding regarding troubled youth and prevention of delinquency; transfer of knowledge to promote social responsibility; financial efficiency; and better use of limited agency resources.

Intergenerational programming allows opportunities of self-fulfillment where everyone wins by demonstrating that each generation can offer and share something that involves time, talent, and resources. Recreation programs can fill the social and self-fulfillment needs of people. Positive recreational social experiences can combat urban social problems like loneliness and isolation.

In comparison with the other 49 states, the Iowa population base contains the third highest percentage of senior citizens in the U.S. (See Table 3).

Table 3: Older Adult Population—Iowa vs. U.S.

In comparison to the general population of the United States:

- Iowa has the highest percentage of older adults over the age of 85 (2%);

- Iowa ranks #2 in older adult population over the age of 75 (7%);

- Iowa ranks #3 in older adult population over age 65 (15%); and

- Iowa ranks #4 in older adult population over age 60 (20%).

Source: *1990 U.S. Census.* Washington, DC: U.S. Government Printing Office.

West Des Moines is a suburban community populated primarily by young, upwardly mobile families which have children living far from their grandparents. In response to these issues and evolving realities, the West Des Moines Department of Parks and Recreation decided to shift programming efforts from focusing on age-segregated programs to establishing integrated programs to unite participants in various age groups. One of the first programs of this type organized grandparent-grandchild bus trips to local and regional attractions. However, this program proved limited in scope and other options were sought.

II. Vision

The vision of the Department was to create a positive link between young and old participants with win-win activities for everyone involved. The Read-to-Me program evolved to match third grade students with senior citizens who wished to share a love of reading. The program would involve children reading to seniors, and seniors reading to children in a format designed to encourage interaction rather than simple entertainment. The Department selected reading because its staff was participating in a broad-based community literacy program. In contrast to the grandparent-grandchild bus trips program, few, if any, of the participants were related. This is an important distinction considering the large number of children and senior citizens in the community who have no relatives from these generations living nearby.

The concept linked several agencies for program delivery efforts which allowed for a pool of resources and utilization of specialized expertise: West Des Moines Parks and Recreation, West Des Moines Community Education, West Des Moines Schools, Border's Book Shop, Friends of West Des Moines Public Library, and nine area nursing homes.

III. Objectives

As originally conceptualized, institutionalized senior citizens were expected to be the primary beneficiaries of the program, but it soon became evident that benefits would also affect the younger participants. The Department developed six objectives, several of which reflect the reciprocal nature of the program's anticipated benefits:

1. To provide opportunities for children to see that, like themselves, senior citizens have feelings and need love; to provide opportunities for the seniors to see that, like themselves, children have feelings and need love.

2. To provide opportunities for the children to see that, like themselves, seniors are capable and special; to provide opportunities for the seniors to see that, like themselves, children are capable and special.

3. To provide opportunities for the children and seniors to experience self-fulfillment by enhancing other people's lives.

4. To develop "a community feeling" within the children as they recognize, accept and fulfill their responsibilities to the elderly community.

5. To provide the opportunity for children to build confidence in their ability to read aloud.

6. To provide a service to an underserved population (i.e., nursing home residents) which was not previously targeted by Department programs. The two exceptions were the Department sponsored, annual Christmas Light Tours, and the Annual Picnic, a one-day event which began in 1975. However, Read-to-Me represented the first Departmental program to be held in nursing homes.

IV. Management Paradigms Shift

Two agencies (West Des Moines Schools, and the West Des Moines Parks and Recreation Department) had an ongoing relationship, so this program was a natural outgrowth of shared goals. Read-to-Me was the first joint programming effort between the Parks and Recreation Department with the West Des Moines Library and the Friends of the Library group, a fledgling organization.

Staff from the Department of Parks and Recreation and West Des Moines Community Education initiated the idea. These two groups selected the third grade students because their curriculum included a component about aging issues and the third graders were considered mature enough to adjust to the challenges of the program. Dovetailing with school curriculum helped the two founding agencies promote the program among school teachers. All twenty-six third-grade teachers in the West Des Moines District were invited to participate: twenty-four responded positively in the first year (1991), and all twenty-six participated the second year (1992).

V. Key Players

Initiators included the Recreation Supervisor, West Des Moines Parks and Recreation, Director of Community Service Learning, and West Des Moines Community Education. As the program formed, activity directors from nine area nursing homes, the teachers, and homeroom volunteers gave input.

In the second year, the Friends of the West Des Moines Public Library became involved by serving as volunteers during the site visits, thus relieving Parks and Recreation staff for other time commitments. Input from the children who participated during the first year was also reviewed in the second year's planning process.

VI. Processes Undertaken to Accomplish Change

Third-grade classes were assigned to nursing homes primarily based on location and ease of transportation. The schools provided transportation for the project, but Community Education and the Department of Parks and Recreation financed it. The city's library lacked sufficient materials for long-term loans to sustain the project, but assistance came from other participants. Border's Book Shop donated materials suitable for the project both in terms of subject matter and the reading skills of the third-grade students. The employees of the Department of Parks and Recreation and Border's Book Shop coordinated many of these efforts that evolved into the "bag of books" for the program.

Community education staff developed class materials to help teachers prepare their students for participation in the program and to assist the children in interpreting and reflecting on their experiences. One purpose of the class materials was to help the children be as comfortable as possible in the nursing home environment and with senior citizens before their visits. Children were told basic rules about nursing home settings, and were taught how to handle situations that might arise, such as what to do if one of the elderly participants fell asleep during a session.

Initially children went to the individual senior citizens' rooms, which proved uncomfortable for many of the participants, especially the children. Therefore, the program format was quickly modified so that nursing home activity directors assisted by gathering residents in common rooms readied for their visitors. The activity directors and teachers assigned children and seniors to dyads and small groups. This format proved to be popular with both the children and the senior citizens. Some nursing home directors offered refreshments which were appreciated, especially by the children. The refreshments helped serve as an icebreaker between the two groups. The children were also encouraged to bring a small gift, such as a picture or a valentine, to give to the seniors.

VII. Marketing to Internal and/or External Publics

Little marketing effort was required to promote the program internally. Both client groups (i.e., schools and nursing homes) supported the program from the outset. Most formal efforts involved documenting the outcome for external publics. These efforts included a slide show prepared by a volunteer for the Park Board, School Board and other interested groups. Publicity for the program generated into a human-interest story published in the *Des Moines Register*, and an article titled "Intergenerational Reading Program Proves Successful" in the December 1992 issue of *Marketing Recreation Classes*. The Department now supplements the slide show with a video presentation of the program.

VIII. Impact of Change on the Agency

This program represented an exploratory effort for serving an underserved population (e.g., nursing home residents) that was not traditionally targeted by the Department of Parks and Recreation. It also provided a successful model for future cooperative efforts between agencies. The annual cost of $500 for transportation provided by the Park and Recreation Department proved the program to be cost-effective since the program serves more that 500 students and 1,848 nursing home residents.

The successes of the Grandparent-Grandchildren Bus Trips and Read-to-Me programs spurred development of additional Department of Parks and Recreation intergenerational programs: an annual senior prom where senior citizens and high school seniors gather together at a dance; grant research provides library funding to purchase additional reading material for the Read-to-Me program; and "Mentors, Inc." The Mentors, Inc. program began in the summer of 1993 when seven participants in the Iowa Senior Games paired with young people who have similar event interests. Like the Read-to-Me program, participants in the Mentors, Inc. program received some pre-event training and information so that participants from each generation would be sensitive to the needs and behaviors of the other group.

IX. Impact of Change on the Community

This demonstration of a successful intergenerational program set the stage for additional Departmental efforts. Initial indications of benefits realized by both the youth and the elderly are positive. After the shyness between participants dissipates, a special bonding occurs in a very short time. Documentation of the short-term and long-term effects of these programs represent both a challenge and a priority.

X. Measurement of the Outcome

The Read-to-Me program received external recognition in the form of two awards: the 1992 Community Involvement in Education Award sponsored by the Iowa Community Education Association; and the Iowa Department of Education and the Iowa Youth Volunteer Award sponsored by the Iowa Department of Economic Development. The Read-to-Me program received the latter award at the Governor's Annual Volunteer Recognition Ceremony which provided the Department with positive statewide publicity.

Internal evaluative efforts are still being developed and refined. Teachers evaluated the first- and second-year programs based on their own opinions and comments gathered informally from the children. In the past year, teachers received evaluations at the initial organizational meeting for the program. Activity directors provided feedback from the nursing homes following the children's visit. Plans for the third year include the development of formal evaluation procedures involving both the children and the senior citizens. Files of letters containing feedback and comments from children, parents, and nursing home residents are being compiled. Beyond statistics and evaluations, the outcome of this program is measured in smiles, hugs, tears—all expressions of positive experiences. The quotes in Table 4 provide insight into those experiences.

Table 4: Quotes of Program Participants

From students:	"I was kind of anxious about going first, but it was one of the neatest activities we've done all year."
From teachers:	"The children were able to talk with and learn about elderly people. Not only did the children share about themselves, but also they learned about someone else's life. Some children commented on the sadness that they felt, because their new friend received so few visitors."
	"Children were amazed that the residents were so appreciative of their visit."
	"I had a boy who had no self-confidence. He practiced reading his story many times; his new friend kept complementing his reading. When he got back to the classroom he asked to read to the entire class."
From advisors:	"It was very gratifying to see the loving smiles and the caring listening that invaded the room when the children came to share story time with my residents. I witnessed a new side to the people that I work with every day."

Author's Suggested Readings and References

1990 U.S. Census. (1990). Washington, DC: U.S. Government Printing Office.

Gerleman, P. (1992, December). Intergenerational reading program proves successful. *Marketing Recreation Classes.*

Gerleman, P. (1993, June). Access for intergenerational programs. *Marketing Recreation Classes*, p. 5.

Hawthorne, V. (1992, March 16). Small voice a big joy to seniors. *Des Moines Register*, p. 7A.

Larson, C. (1993, July). Creating connections: Intergenerational programs. *Programmers Information Network*, 4(3), pp. 1-2. National Recreation and Park Association.

Sociodemographic Characteristics—

Indianapolis

Indianapolis, Indiana

1990 Population:
731,327

Median Age:
31.6

Household Composition:
78.9% in families

Chapter 9

Indiana Sports Corporation and Its Partnerships

Indianapolis, Indiana

Jim Titus
Vice President of Operations, and
Executive Director of White River Park State Games
Indiana Sports Corporation

I. The Situation

Near the end of the 1970s the City of Indianapolis, after a period of little to no growth, acquired a sleepy image and nicknames such as "India-no-place" and "Naptown." The downtown district was not a ghost town, but it was clearly underutilized relative to its potential. Many of the city's leaders began to investigate various options the community might pursue in order to increase not only the city's image but also its tools for economic development. After many months of discussion, amateur sports became the vehicle for the transformation of Indianapolis from India-no-place to a city on the move.

Certainly, it was imperative for the City of Indianapolis to initiate changes in order to better its national image as well as begin the economic revitalization process. The Indiana Sports Corporation (ISC), founded in 1979, assisted the city in its quest for redevelopment and established Indianapolis as the first major "player" city to use amateur sports as a tool for a proposed economic turn-around. A vision was set for the city. By way of the partnerships that developed between ISC and many other entities, Indianapolis became a focal point for what can happen when people, government and business work together.

II. Vision

Primarily, the vision was to turn Indianapolis into a leading national city by bringing not only spectators to town for various competitions, but also to lure new business via enhanced growth and opportunities that would be available because of the emphasis placed on sports. Unsure of the visionaries' original expectations of what the city's economy and overall image would look like ten to twelve years down the road, a large portion of the vision was met. The next step was to enhance upon what the city acquired and to continue economic and social growth via the sport mechanism.

III. Objectives

The Indiana Sports Corporation (ISC) developed three objectives:

1. To create a positive dynamic image for Indianapolis among both its own citizens and nonresidents.

2. To use sport as an economic development tool.

3. To develop opportunities for new businesses.

IV. Management Paradigm Shift

The initial composition of the management group was already diversified in areas that were necessary to reach its goals and objectives. However, basic to the plan was the maintenance of ISC-facilitated partnerships at all times to assure that each group involved stayed informed about what everyone else was doing.

V. Key Players

Members of various private and public groups were involved. Some of these groups were the ISC, the Lilly Endowment, the Capital Improvements Board, various facility managers, hotels and motels, the Mayor's office, and a number of private entities.

Eli Lilly Corporation is one of the major employers in Indianapolis. The Lilly Endowment funds projects, primarily in Indiana, related to advancing community, religious, and educational development.

The Capital Improvements Board is a city agency responsible for managing major public facilities including the Hoosier Dome and the Indianapolis Convention Center.

VI. Processes Undertaken to Accomplish Change

The process actually began in the mid-1970s with a needs assessment for the City of Indianapolis. The needs assessment focused on potential vehicles for improving the City's image and economic opportunity structure, and on how best to initiate the process of improvement. The group of city leaders listed previously spearheaded the needs assessment. Several informal groups contributed input for the process including a group of civic leaders who met weekly as the Tuesday Afternoon Club; a second group of civic leaders called the City Committee; and a group of business leaders called the Corporate Community Council.

Although options for revitalizing and courting the traditional manufacturing industry were considered, the City recognized that heavy industry was on a decline. Many proponents of change seized on the possibility to enhance Indianapolis' service industry potential. The City's central geographic location, both within the State of Indiana and in the United States, became an asset as plans developed. The vehicle for change became amateur sports with the formation of the Indiana Sports Corporation. Staffing was modest as it consisted of two employees: the president and an administrative assistant.

The next step was to figure out how the city would position itself in order to reach its goals. The first major set of projects was the construction of various world class venue sites around the city. The Major Taylor Velodrome (1982), Indiana University Natatorium on the campus of IUPUI (1982), Indianapolis Tennis Center (1979), and the IUPUI Track and Field Stadium (1982) represented the projects completed in the early 1980s. Facility managers were sought not only for their expertise in managing the facilities on a daily basis, but also to run events at the level Indianapolis proposed (e.g., the city's long-term focus on major events like the U.S. Olympic Trials). A review process developed to enable ISC, its partner agencies and businesses to evaluate and bid on those events which could easily meet the established goals and objectives.

Prior to the 1979 inception of ISC, the City successfully bid for the 1982 National Sports Festival (Olympic Festival). For this first scheduled event that would involve the city's public and private sections as well as ISC, the need for solid organization was recognized and met. The 1982 event, regarded as the most successful Sports Festival up to its time, put Indianapolis on the map as an up and coming community. However, the mission of ISC was conceived as a long-term proposition. It was not developed simply to organize the Sport Festival and then fade into oblivion.

ISC often takes the lead in initiating bids and soliciting potential events for the City, but many of the ideas originate from within affiliated agencies, organizations, and businesses. The ISC Events Committee researches, compiles data, and screens various proposed events to determine which events are consistent with the City's objectives to provide maximum economic and quality of life benefits for the residents of Indianapolis. Since 1982, ISC and the City have organized and hosted over 300 national or international amateur sporting events. Some of the highest profile events included:

- NCAA Final Four (1991)
- Diving Olympic Trials (1992)
- Swimming Olympic Trials (1992)
- Tenth Pan Am Games (1987)
- Olympic Track & Field Trials (1988)
- World Gymnastics Championships (1991)

VII. Marketing to Internal and/or External Publics

Since its inception, a concerted effort was made by ISC to promote the City and bring various sporting events to Indianapolis. The variety of means used began with local media (e.g., television, radio, newsprint). Consequently, once the city's reputation began to grow, the national and international press began to write or broadcast information about the city and its accomplishments. Their story was recounted to companies and interest groups around the state and nation. The popularity of athletics tends to spread on its own and, with the emphasis Indianapolis placed on amateur sports, the city began to develop the image the visionaries sought. That image presented Indianapolis as a safe and clean city to visit. Indianapolis also became known as an inexpensive relocation choice for businesses and families. Obvious to the promotional effort was repetition involving the above mentioned amenities that Indianapolis offered. Indianapolis enjoys a "first with the most" reputation with respect to amateur sporting organizations. That is, Indianapolis was the first city actively to seek out and nurture ongoing relationships with amateur sports organizations. As a result, the city has attracted more such organizations than has any other U.S. city.

One challenge facing the City in the immediate future is the rising cost of living caused, in part, by the success of the past revitalization efforts. Indianapolis' cost of living is now comparable to cities of similar size (e.g., Portland, Cincinnati, Louisville) whereas it was lower just a few years ago.

VIII. Impact of Change on Agency

The most important impact the success of amateur sports had on ISC was staffing needs. The staff of ISC grew substantially over the years—from the 1979 level of two full-time employees, to ten in 1985, to its 1994 complement of 25. ISC revenues come primarily from three sources: event revenues, memberships (both individual and corporate), and private funding (e.g., foundation grants). Revenues, though not paralleling the increase in staff, grew substantially for the organization.

Over 1,000 corporate members and between 800 and 1,500 individual members support ISC. Corporate memberships averaged $1,000 apiece on an annual basis, but most individual memberships fall in the $50-$100 range.

In some cases, such as major events, ISC assumes a direct provider role. One of ISC's main missions however, is to offer facilitative services for little or no fee. For example, when the City of Indianapolis expressed an interest in improving its relations with the Big Ten Conference, ISC sponsored a Big Ten luncheon in Indianapolis. In other cases ISC provides support services, such as coordinating media efforts for small events. ISC wishes to maintain its cooperative-oriented philosophy with various businesses and other related entities in the area. The success that ISC and the City realized over the past several years resulted from forming long-term partnerships by nature.

The expertise ISC accumulated through its involvement in sporting events enabled it to develop an efficient bid and event management process. For example, when ISC bid for the 2000 NCAA Final Four, it planned for the procedures needed to work with the press, the layout of the Hoosier Dome facility, and arranged for street closings and extra parking arrangements. It also has a huge database of contacts upon which to draw. Indianapolis and ISC became a model for other national cities that are planning to use sports as a development tool.

IX. Impact of Change on Community

One impact of the amateur sports movement on Indianapolis is the number of sports National Governing Bodies (NGBs) that relocated their organizations to this community. These organizations, most which relocated between 1980 and 1989, include:

- U.S. Gymnastics
- U.S. Diving, Inc.
- U.S. Synchronized Swimming
- USA Track & Field
- U.S. Rowing
- U.S. Canoe & Kayak
- U.S. Water Polo
- Amateur Athletic Union
- National Institute of Fitness & Sport
- American College of Sports Medicine
- National Association of Government Councils on Physical Fitness and Sport

In addition, one international federation, the International Baseball Association, now calls Indianapolis its home.

Second, the whole Indianapolis service industry became more efficient about how it conducts business. Hotels, motels, restaurants, and retail outlets now work closely with ISC. The experience gained by these entities benefits the overall presentation that the City provides during large or small sporting events.

Finally, recent research confirmed that amateur sports provided socio-economic benefits to the area over the past several years. Schaffer and Associates (1993) collected personal-interview and survey-based data from 31 amateur sports organizations, special events, and facilities based in Indianapolis. As a result, the City accumulated detailed information regarding event attendance, employment, revenues (including sources), and expenditures (including uses). The data compiled by Schaffer et al. (1993) reveal that between 1977 and 1991:

- eighteen amateur sports organizations brought $213 million into the Indianapolis economy from outside sources and provided 237 jobs;

- the nine major sports facilities brought $51 million into the City's economy from outside sources and provided 289 jobs during that same time period;

- attendance at the 330 major amateur sports events hosted from 1977 to 1991 totaled 4.53 million spectators and 215,000 participants; and

- approximately 68 percent of the spectators and 76 percent of the participants came from outside the City. Their spending totaled $787 million during that time period.

Table 5:   Returns on Investment

Returns on investment were also calculated for the 1977-1991 time period on three levels:

Investment	Return	ROI	Entity
$35.1 M	$62.6 M (Taxes)	23%	City Government
$8.1 M	$81.4 M (Taxes)	65%	State Government
$164.0 M	$683.0 M (Residents' Income)	64%	Total (includes private sector)

X. Measurement of Outcome

One of the main devices used recently to measure the success of the amateur sports movement is economic impact detailed in Table 5. The Indianapolis Chamber of Commerce also published studies on ISC programs' impact on youth sports and fitness, and residents' perceptions of sports' impact on quality of life. Youth-related issues are covered in detail in Chapter Ten and, therefore, will not be discussed here. Gentlemen Associates (1993) conducted research regarding how the City's amateur sports strategy affected quality of life in the community. Three groups were focused on and an additional 400 residents were interviewed by telephone in 1992. Population samples represented the full spectrum of the City's population, and the results are accurate within a margin of error of plus or minus five percent.

Gentlemen (1993) found that 59 percent of Indianapolis' residents believed that the quality of life in the City changed for the better over the past fifteen years as compared to 28 percent who believed that the quality of life changed for the worse. Those with high levels of income and education possessed the most positive attitudes. Nearly half (48 percent) of the county's residents participated in at least one of the amateur sports events held during the past few years, as spectators, volunteers and/or hosts of out-of-town visitors. Middle-aged, upper income and well-educated individuals were overrepresented among participants. More than 80 percent of the City's residents were aware of the amateur sports strategy. Of those who were aware of Indianapolis' amateur sports strategy, 91 percent felt that it is successful as compared with five percent who felt it unsuccessful. This high level of support was consistent among all socioeconomic groups. More than 90 percent of the residents believed that the strategy should be pursued in the future. Most residents felt that the greatest impact of the program had been in improving perceptions of Indianapolis among nonresidents.

Another method used in follow-up studies was conducted with the entities with which ISC works during an event (e.g., the Big Ten Office, U.S. Gymnastics). Generally, ISC takes a lead role in generating feedback regarding events; information which is then shared with cooperating agencies and businesses. The follow-up details areas of efficiency as well as trouble points. These reports are critical in evaluating future events and those services to be offered.

A final indication of ISC's success is the growing number of sporting associations, both in large cities (e.g., Dallas, Houston, Minneapolis, Phoenix, San Diego), and in smaller cities (e.g., Fort Wayne and Bloomington, Indiana). ISC adopted consultative and facilitative roles, especially with associations in other Indiana cities to help them bid for smaller region-based events that prefer more intimate settings offered in the smaller cities.

Author's Suggested Readings and References

Gentleman, K. L. (1993). *Beyond the games: Residents respond*. Indianapolis, IN: Indianapolis Chamber of Commerce.

Kriplen, N. (1993). *Beyond the games: A history*. Indianapolis, IN: Indianapolis Chamber of Commerce.

National Institute for Fitness and Sport. (1992). *Beyond the games: Impact on youth sports and fitness*. Indianapolis, IN: Lilly Endowment, Inc.

Schaffer, W. A., Jaffee, B. L., and Davidson, L. S. (1993). *Beyond the games: The economic impact of amateur sports in Indianapolis, 1977-91*. Indianapolis, IN: Indianapolis Chamber of Commerce.

Sociodemographic Characteristics—

Indianapolis

Indianapolis, Indiana

1990 Population:

731,327

Median Age:

31.6

Household Composition:

78.9% in families

Chapter 10

Indy ProKids Youth Sports Initiative: Indiana Sports Corporation

Indianapolis, Indiana

Debra Turner
Vice President of Youth Sports Initiatives and Community Relations
Indiana Sports Corporation

I. The Situation

Since 1979, Indiana Sports Corporation (ISC) attracted more than 300 national and international sporting events to central Indiana. ISC, created to attract these major amateur sporting events, assists with the coordination and promotion of the events. By targeting sports as a growth industry for Indianapolis, ISC is recognized as the industry leader in sports and, during its first decade, achieved success through developing and hosting athletic events. ISC initiated an effort in late 1989 to develop a strategic plan to guide the organization into its second decade. This strategic planning group, led by a local business person and the staff of ISC, included ten community leaders. The committee conducted interviews with fifty people involved in government, sports, civic, and business organizations.

As a result of the eighteen-month study completed in 1991, the group developed a strategic plan for ISC to promote the development of Indianapolis and Indiana through sport. That development is intended to:

1. Stimulate local economies by developing a permanent sports industry presence in Indianapolis, and attract, host or assist amateur sporting events.

2. Improve the image of Indianapolis by further development of the City's reputation as a leader in the sports industry.

3. Enhance the quality of life in Indiana communities by providing a wide range of first class spectator, participant, and volunteer sporting opportunities.

4. Improve the opportunity for Indiana's youth to be involved in well-run sporting events as both participants and spectators.

In order to be judged successful, each development area must be accessible to all members of the Indianapolis area communities who desire to participate in them. However, no constituency served by the ISC is considered more important than youth. Institutions which traditionally provided sports opportunities to youth lost their capability to do so for a variety of reasons related to socioeconomic changes and economic constraints. For example, physical education programs in many school districts are offered for as little as two hours per week. In response to this trend and to the latter two goals described above, ISC increased its efforts in the area of youth programming. The Center for Early Adolescence (CEA) advocates seven developmental needs of youth. These needs provide a framework from which ISC youth programming evolved:

1. Young people need a wide variety of experiences.

2. Young people need chances to explore and define who they are and how they relate to others.

3. Young people need to participate in meaningful activities.

4. Young people need to interact positively with their peers and with adults.

5. Young people need plenty of physical activity.

6. Young people need opportunities to do well and to have their achievements acknowledged.

7. Young people need structure and limits.

The ISC elected to concentrate on three types of programs. The first focal point provided participatory opportunities for the State's youth such as the White River Park State Games. The Games are an Olympic-style event that features competition in 21 different sports. In the past ten years, the number of Games participants rose from just over 5,000 to more than 9,000 annually and the number of spectators climbed from roughly 8,000 people to 30,000 people annually.

ISC's second focus is on events that involve auxiliary programs that benefit youth, such as sports clinics or in-school education programs conducted in association with various national and international competitions. For example, the Circle City Classic is a youth football clinic held annually in conjunction with a championship level game between two traditionally African-American universities at the Hoosier Dome. The NFL Players Association Retired Players sponsors this event which features retired NFL players, current high school coaches, and players from selected area high school football teams to serve as mentors for the young clinic participants.

The third focus is on efforts which raise funds to directly benefit youth programs. For example, $1.9 million was raised by Youthlinks Indiana and Larry Bird's All-Star Classic since 1988. Youthlinks is a celebrity golf tournament, held each June, where celebrities and corporate representatives form six-somes to raise money for youth sports programs. The NFL Players Association Retired Players also conducted a golf tournament in 1994 which raised enough money to buy football helmets for six middle-schools. The schools only offered flag football in previous years because they lacked proper equipment for full-contact football.

The focus of most youth-based efforts is statewide, although most of the programs were pilot-tested in central Indiana. ISC sought a program that would focus permanently on the Indianapolis community.

II. Vision

ISC envisioned an enterprise whereby the assets of the City of Indianapolis, including both people and facilities, would be systematically tapped to expand and enhance sports activities for youth. Indianapolis is the home of four professional sports teams: the National Basketball Association's Indiana Pacers, the National Football League's Indianapolis Colts, the American [baseball] Association's Indianapolis Indians, and the International Hockey League's Indianapolis Ice.

Professional athletes can carry tremendous influence in the minds of youth. Many children idolize their favorite professional sport figure. For example, if Michael Jordan eats Wheaties for breakfast, then little John Smith wants to eat Wheaties for breakfast. If Michael Jordan wears Nike basketball shoes, then little John Smith wants to wear Nike basketball shoes.

These influences occur on the national level, but few youth have any opportunities to see their favorite athletes compete in-person, let alone interact with their favorite athletic personality. However, at a local level, professional athletes can serve as positive role models for youth by reaching out through organized efforts to enhance grassroots youth sports programming. ISC envisioned professional athletes working with youth in many fundamental situations. Thus, the Indy ProKids (Professionals Reaching Out; Kids Involved Doing Sports) program was established. ProKids uses the unique collaborative efforts of Indianapolis' four professional sports teams.

III. Objectives

ISC established four objectives for ProKids:

1. To increase youth participation in well-organized sports activities.

2. To encourage participation in sports activities and develop positive influences while children enjoy sports.

3. To offer professional athletes an opportunity to get involved with the community that supports their athletic efforts.

4. To offer professional athletes a chance to be positive role models for youth, regardless of the sports team or professional level with which they are affiliated.

IV. Management Paradigm Shift

ISC initiated the effort for the four professional sports teams in Indianapolis to work together to benefit youth. This type of collaboration is not as common as might be supposed. As a rule, management personnel of the various teams did not know each other well. The teams' seasons obviously differ so that personnel are in and out of town at different times of the year, and the busy season for one sport is often a slow season for another sport. In addition, the teams represent two different levels of sport. The Colts and Pacers represent the highest professional level available in football and basketball respectively, whereas the Indians and Ice are top level minor league franchises for the Cincinnati Reds [baseball] and the Chicago Blackhawks [hockey]. In sum, cooperative efforts among professional teams representing different sports and different levels are rare.

V. Key Players

An Indy ProKids Advisory Committee formed with one management representative and one professional athlete representative from each team. Three representatives from ISC and one representative from the Indianapolis Department of Parks and Recreation (Indy Parks) were also on the committee.

VI. Processes Undertaken to Accomplish Change

ISC created its Youth Sports Initiatives and Community Relations division in 1992 and hired a division director in August of that year. Soon after, in November 1992, the Director began recruiting members for the youth sports advisory committee from the athletes and management staff of the City's professional teams. Over the next several months, a full menu of opportunities for professional athlete involvement was presented to members of (what is now titled) the Indy ProKids Advisory Committee. Team representatives highlighted various opportunities in which their team members would feel comfortable participating. In one instance, a program was already established by a team acting independently. Other programs were developed cooperatively by various teams and ISC. For example, the Colts sponsor Coats for Kids, a program which encourages fans to bring old coats to the stadium on game day. The Indians sponsor a program titled Anthem Buddies. Through this program, members of youth sports teams run onto the field alongside Indian players before games and stand with the players for the national anthem. The Indians also have a special seating section for teams and individual youth who signed anti-drug pledge forms. These individual efforts will continue on behalf of particular teams. However, other opportunities were made available for player involvement through Indy ProKids. The Pacers sponsored a Youth Jam Session in conjunction with the 1994 NBA Draft. Participants watched and competed in skills demonstrations and competitions including one-on-one, free-throw accuracy, dunking, and obstacle courses.

On average, each of the City's four professional teams sponsor two ProKids-related programs a season. The ISC Advisory Committee identified opportunities that could be developed for all teams to participate, and opportunities that were outside the realm of professional sports contacts.

Some traditional opportunities were not possible. For example, fundraisers featuring the Colts versus Indians in a basketball challenge were prevented by player contracts that forbid players to participate in organized sports outside of their own. However, multiteam special events were developed. For example, the ProKids Alley Event, held in conjunction with the Indianapolis 500 Festival, is an annual downtown event involving all four franchises. A block-long section of street is closed off and each professional team sends representatives to guide participating youth through a series of skills exercises: pitching a baseball at a target while being timed with a pitching gun measures both accuracy and velocity of the kids' arms (Indians); entering slam-dunk and free-throw competitions (Pacers); throwing footballs through moving and stationary tires (Colts); and playing street hockey (Ice).

In 1995 Indianapolis hosted the national convention of NFL Players Association Retired Players. ISC planned several community activities for youth in conjunction with this event. Retired players are excellent role models for youth because many are still young, yet had to make adjustments to nonathletic careers. Retired players are especially convincing regarding the need to develop academic and career skills that will be useful outside of professional sports arenas.

VII. Marketing to Internal and/or External Publics

Promotional efforts are essential to the success of ProKids. In February 1993, a press conference was held by the Indy ProKids Advisory Committee and the Mayor of Indianapolis to introduce ProKids to the broader community. The press conference was held at an Indy Parks recreation center where youth groups participate in a basketball program. The professional athletes and their management representatives, together with the Director of Indy Parks and Director of Youth Sports Initiatives, presented a component of the Indy ProKids program. In turn, the Mayor commended the unprecedented collaboration effort of the four professional sports teams to directly benefit youth. Local media coverage carried the message to the public. In addition, several follow-up articles were written to outline this unique relationship.

All ProKids programs are offered free of charge to assure maximum accessibility, especially for youth from low-income households. ProKids events are either subsidized directly by one of the professional franchises or with money collected from some of the aforementioned fundraisers. Many ProKids programs are community-wide events open to everyone, however admission to some specialized clinics is restricted in order to maintain adequate mentor/coach-youth ratios. Most clinics have enrollment capacities of about 200 participants. In cases such as these, youth organizations are selected on a rotating basis. ProKids programs established a high profile in the Indianapolis community so waiting lists are common.

Distribution issues are also a continuing concern because of the central locations of most ProKids programs, the relative lack of mobility among ProKids' target markets, and the fact that many programs are targeted to at-risk and low income youth. With respect to program location, ProKids events can rarely be brought to individual neighborhoods or communities because they are generally part of larger events held at major facilities such as the Hoosier Dome. As stated earlier, one of ISC's central missions is to promote major sporting events, not draw people away from them to other venues. ISC staff recently reached an agreement with the Metro bus system to alleviate access problems for youth with limited transportation options. The bus system, as a community service, offers vouchers to and from ProKids events. Young children are permitted to ride free in the company of an adult, and middle-school-age and older youths are given free passes to ride on their own.

In addition to improved access to ProKids events, the program has the added benefits of educating youth about etiquette in public situations and conveying to drivers that the City's youth are clients too.

VIII. Impact of the Change on Agency

Indy ProKids is the first highly visible effort of Youth Sports Initiatives to utilize the city's assets for the benefit of the community's youth. Indy ProKids relationships with the four professional sports teams, and an improved understanding of ISC's mission and goals broadcasts to a more diverse population.

As the professional players got more involved, the players themselves became the advocates for the program, and encouraged additional involvement from the other athletes. It is interesting to note that many of the athletes from other professional sports in the same city have not had the opportunity to interact and consequently few are acquainted with one another.

IX. Impact of Change on the Community

Although the Indy ProKids program is in its infancy, the positive impact of this program caused increased participation in various youth sports programs. Positive change through the initial publicity of Indy ProKids led to an additional relationship with a fifth professional sports entity in Indianapolis; a newly established chapter of the NFL Players Association Retired Players is forming in Indianapolis. This chapter, under the leadership of such former stars as Mark Hermann, John Isenbarger and Blair Kiel, is anxious and enthusiastic about participating at all levels of the Indy ProKids program. This developing relationship is a major benefit to the ProKids program. The NFL Players Association Retired Players chapter already sponsored a youth clinic in the Hoosier Dome.

X. Measurement of the Outcome

The success of the Indy ProKids program will be judged using two criteria: (1) the increased rate of youth participation in ProKids sponsored programs, and (2) positive satisfaction with sports activities in the Indy ProKids program. To date, satisfaction with ProKids programs was measured indirectly by the fact that the ISC has waiting lists for programs and is no longer required to solicit participation from other organized youth organizations. In the future, it is expected that a more formal data collection effort will be undertaken as part of the ISC's efforts to evaluate itself.

Author's Suggested Readings and References

Gentleman, K. L. (1993). *Beyond the games: Residents respond.* Indianapolis, IN: Indianapolis Chamber of Commerce.

Kriplen, N. (1993). *Beyond the games: A history.* Indianapolis, IN: Indianapolis Chamber of Commerce.

National Institute for Fitness and Sport. (1992). *Beyond the games: Impact on youth sports and fitness.* Indianapolis, IN: Lilly Endowment, Inc.

Schaffer, W. A., Jaffee, B. L., and Davidson, L. S. (1993). *Beyond the games: The economic impact of amateur sports in Indianapolis, 1977-91.* Indianapolis, IN: Indianapolis Chamber of Commerce.

Sociodemographic Characteristics—

Waco, Texas

1990 Population:
103,590

Median Age:
28.9

Household Composition:
71.6% in families

Chapter 11

Reinventing Recreation Programming: Waco Leisure Services Department

Waco, Texas

Sally Gavlik
Recreation Superintendent
Waco Leisure Services Department

I. The Situation

Waco, like many other American cities, faced a host of complex social problems in recent years. As the 1980s came to a close, Waco could claim the highest school dropout and the highest teen pregnancy rates among Texas cities. In addition, it ranked nineteenth in the United States for the percentage of children living below the poverty rate. Park and recreation agencies often assume partial responsibility for providing positive experiences to at-risk youth. However, little evidence suggested that the Waco Leisure Services Department had effectively addressed community problems. Some members of the Department were dissatisfied with their minimal contribution to at-risk youth and the community and, therefore, initiated an internal audit regarding the Department's effectiveness.

In 1989, the Waco Leisure Services Department's Recreation Division operated three recreation centers, a tennis facility, one swimming pool and two senior centers. Programming was limited to opening the facilities' doors to the public. No provision for structured or community outreach programs existed, and often there was little or no participation at the facilities. Fewer than 5,000 people came to the City's recreation centers per year and the municipal swimming pool attracted fewer than 25 visitors each day. Budgets had been cut drastically in 1982 and 1985. These two cuts eliminated between 30 and 40 percent of the Department's operating budget. Many programs shifted to other agencies and much of the staff was eliminated in the Leisure Services Department. Capital maintenance budgets for parks and recreation facilities were nonexistent since the early 1980s. In summary, the recreation and parks facilities suffered from a lack of repair and cleanliness, and were underutilized by the public.

The recreation division staff restructured in 1989 to include a Recreation Superintendent and Community Outreach Specialist. In 1990, an Athletic

Supervisor was added to the staff and, in 1992 a Special Event Coordinator joined the team. The staff changes were designed to upgrade and expand services. The Parks Division initiated a parallel restructuring in 1991. The primary goal for the Department was to upgrade all facilities, services, and programs.

II. Vision

Members of the Leisure Services Department originally proposed the impetus for change. The Brazos Coordinating Committee (BCC) was also involved in formulating the change strategy. The BCC was formed in 1989 from members of seven City departments: Leisure Services, Convention and Visitors Services, Economic Development, Police, Management Services, Finance, and the City Manager's office. The BCC was created to assist economic development along Waco's section of the Brazos River. A corridor was designed for park and recreational activities with a river walk, two major park areas, a recreation center and incorporates a historic suspension bridge. Economic development activities evolved around these facilities.

Change advocates envisioned a Department that would be accountable to the public and provide quality programs and activities. Department facilities would be maintained, upgraded, and expanded to meet the needs of the service area. The Department would serve as a leader and coordinate with service agencies (e.g., the Convention and Visitors Bureau, area school districts) to ensure the maximum usage of all available funds, including Community Development Block Grants. The reputation, creditability, and recognition of the Department would be enhanced as it became a proactive leader in the community.

III. Objectives

The Leisure Service Department and BCC developed three objectives:

1. To increase revenue generation through class fees, grants, and sponsorships placed in a separate budget—the Performance Fund. This Fund would supplement funds allocated from the first budget—the General Fund. Performance Fund moneys, under complete control of the Leisure Services Department, were conceived primarily as seed money for special projects. An additional benefit of retaining a separate Performance Fund would be that money saved from the previous fiscal years would not automatically return to the larger City budget.

2. To expand programming at recreation centers and parks, increase outreach initiatives, and enlarge specialty areas such as athletics and special events.

3. To develop a promotional campaign to bring attention to department activities and facilities.

IV. Management Paradigm Shift

The first shift involved changing the recreational programming philosophy from one that provides free drop-in play to one that offers fee-based programs. Second, the Department helped develop special events and facilities specifically designed to generate tourism revenues. Third, the Department abandoned its passive take-it-or-leave-it philosophy, and began to actively promote and advertise the Department's activities and facilities.

V. Key Players

Key players in the change process included a half-dozen high-level administrators within the Leisure Services Department, the Assistant City Manager, the Brazos Corridor Committee (BCC), and the Convention and Visitors Bureau. Ideas related to this change process were most often generated by the Leisure Services Department which restructured its mandate to include Convention and Visitors Services, the BCC, the Planning Department (including neighborhood organizations) and the City Manager's office. All original ideas from these cooperating groups funneled to the Leisure Services Department where specific dollar figures, staffing needs, and facility requirements were addressed. Projects were prioritized based on the goals of City Council and the Department. Funding was provided by both the General and the Performance fund, Community Development Block Grants, foundations, and other grants.

VI. Processes Undertaken to Accomplish Change

The process began in 1989 by a review of existing services and facilities conducted by all Leisure Services staff. For the first time, input and suggestions were solicited from several organized community groups including the Rotary, the Black Chamber of Commerce, churches, and schools. Previously, active groups, such as the Hispanic Chamber of Commerce, were also included. Based on the review, a five-year plan for new programs and maintenance initiatives developed. A capital improvement program evolved to coordinate with the new programs and maintenance initiatives.

A public announcement in June of 1990 stated the results of the planning process and scheduled the starting date on September 1. The new philosophy required more commitment on the part of staff members and placed heavy emphasis on new programs, new budgeting strategies and, for the first time, customer service. Departmental staff lacked unity regarding the change process. Several staff members who could not comprehend the change in philosophy or simply disagreed with the new direction left the Department. Among the departures were all four of the community center supervisors— two resigned and two were fired. Anticipated resistance to the changes from outside the Leisure Services Department never materialized. The Department selected new staff carefully based on their educational and professional experience in recreation and park management. Prior to 1989, newly hired center supervisors did not need a college education or budgeting or programming experience. In the three-year period between 1989 and 1991, seven Recreation Supervisors and a Park Superintendent were hired, and four Park Supervisors were upgraded. The job description for the roving center supervisor position (that had focused on substitution-related duties) was rewritten to include the formation and orchestration of regular community outreach activities targeted to senior citizens and school groups.

Recreation staff reviewed program hours and decided to extend them. The basic criteria for the change in program and facility hours became the preferences of the markets rather than tradition and staff convenience. Prior to the change process, every center operated from 9 a.m. to 6 p.m. The staff expanded the hours to accommodate working parents in the spring and summer. Centers now operate from 7 a.m. to 9 or 10 p.m. Programming is organized and scheduled to avoid inconvenient times. Midmorning hours are reserved for Tiny Tots programs. Friday night's programs are limited in the fall due to Texans' passion for high school football. However, a popular Midnight Basketball program now operates until 2 a.m. on Saturday nights.

The recreation Department initiated agreements with school districts and developed sponsorship proposals. Long-range plans included special events, park upgrades, and new facilities. Particular emphasis for special events was placed on the spring season in order to take advantage of central Texas' mild spring weather. In 1988, a county-wide bond election passed for the construction of a new zoo. This capital project represented the initial step in upgrading the entire Department. Although initiated just prior to the major Departmental overhaul, the zoo project symbolized the holistic approach that characterized rejuvenation efforts. The family-oriented mission of the zoo complemented existing museums in the community that traditionally were oriented toward older crowds. The zoo represented a highly-visible facility to attract both local residents and tourists. It officially opened in July 1993.

The Waco Leisure Service Department developed performance measures to review all existing programs. A park maintenance standardization system was also developed. Programs began on a trial basis, evaluations reviewed, and the programs either expanded or deleted. Programmers had three years to develop and refine programs, after which the programs were retained or deleted. Nothing was considered sacred or above review, not even old programs which had succeeded in the past. For example, roller skating activities, an annual canoe race, and an annual raft race were all cancelled following three unsuccessful start-up efforts. Other programs thrived after modification. Departmental efforts to sponsor children's birthday parties were not successful in their first year. Although changing parental work patterns (e.g., two-income households) and single-parent homes suggested that this type of programming would be popular, program development efforts were insufficient. In the second year, the Department dropped generic unthemed birthday parties, and initiated theme parties based on dinosaurs and zoos. This strategy proved to be much more popular and the birthday party program remains in the Department's plans for the future. Other successful programs include:

Brazos Nights. The Brazos corridor committee developed the first Brazos Nights program in 1989 to generate tourism and activity in the downtown area on weekends. Although virtually never utilized during the evening, the downtown area boasted two beautiful parks and a historic suspension bridge. The event is six weeks long and includes two stages—one for youth and a main stage—and a laser light show. Brazos Nights now maintains an annual attendance of 60,000 people. In the initial years, the program was promoted to area residents, but now has expanded to attract tourists to the Waco area. Originally Brazos Nights ran for twelve weekends but the program's length was shortened to six weekends per year. This change in programming strategy resulted in larger crowds concentrated over fewer days. Financial resources have also been more concentrated, allowing organizers to hire better bands and provide a better laser light show. For four of the six weekends, hotels report a full occupancy rate.

STAR (Start the Afternoons with Recreation). This program began in 1990 as an after school, fee-based enrichment effort targeted at elementary school children from six through twelve years of age. The program operates in conjunction with the school district. Prior to 1990, the school district operated an after-school program that included tutoring and watching television. The Leisure Services Department now supplements the program with a class structure in which youth pay a fee. From the Recreation Division's perspective, this is an outreach program in which staff bring the program to children on-site at the schools. The number of sites increased annually from two schools in the first year to seven in 1993, including five Waco School District sites and two sites operated by other school districts. Programs also expanded to service year-round schools. Year-round schools are only conducted at a few sites. Therefore, these recreational programs are conducted for both year-round and traditional school tracts.

Adopt-A-Trail. This 1993 effort created a program similar to Adopt-A-School or Adopt-A-Park. It has generated activity support to revitalize a trail system which extends from one side of town to the other through a park that connects the downtown area, the new zoo, a college, and the river. The area, once considered dangerous and crime-ridden, now supports numerous weekend activities and is well used by the community.

Softball Program. Waco, one of the originating cities for the Texas Amateur Athletic Federation, boasted over 300 registered teams in the early 1980s which played on a four-field complex and four additional fields located throughout town. In 1985 the program was removed from the City's budget and contracted to the Waco Softball Association, a largely volunteer organization. Unfortunately, this group managed the softball program poorly. Adequate revenues were not returned to the program and the condition of playing fields deteriorated. By 1990, fewer than 100 teams remained in the organization. The Department convinced the City to take back the program, hired appropriate supervision, and maintained the program service. In 1993, more than 200 teams registered, the Department secured seven state tournaments and conducted tournaments for private schools. A new athletic facility is being developed to include softball, tennis, and sand volleyball for the expressed purpose of increasing team registration and securing regional and national tournaments to enhance tourism revenues. This new complex is expected to open in 1996.

VII. Marketing to Internal and/or External Publics

As just described, most of the Leisure Services Department's marketing efforts focused on the program component of the marketing mix. In addition, pricing strategies evolved from the old free, but passive, delivery system into a partially fee-based program system supported by scholarships. Distribution and promotion strategies also evolved. Early into the change process, the eleven full-time Recreation Division staff members recognized that their numbers limited the scope of their potential impact on the 103,000-person community. In order to bolster limited staff resources, the Division proposed employing college students with majors in recreation. They initiated discussion with Baylor University (located in Waco) and several other state universities (e.g., Texas A&M, Texas Tech, Southwest Texas State) that offered recreation or park degrees. This facilitative approach to distributing resources allowed the Recreation Division to maximize its efforts. The Department now hires ten to twenty students annually who work in all areas: recreation, parks, planning, convention, and visitor services. The length of the students' employment varies from summer programs of three months duration to year-long internships. In addition, the Department developed a graduate assistantship with Baylor. Graduate students in this program receive tuition waivers from the University but, rather than work on campus, they work for the Waco Leisure Services Department. This program is expected to increase graduate school registration in addition to providing quality staff for the Department.

Prior to the 1989 change initiative, promotion efforts were minimal. Initially, in 1989 and 1990, the Department published a brochure to advertise activities and park facilities for summer activities only. Since 1991 the brochure has evolved into a professional magazine with advertising, and is printed twice a year. In addition, the brochure and accompanying promotional and registration materials are printed in Spanish to reach the large Hispanic community in Waco.

The Department began to foster a close relationship with the media—something that was not a priority before 1989. Waco Leisure Services incorporates media representatives on all program boards and relies on their expertise. This relationship is fostered annually and is one that the Department does not take for granted. The news media is now notified for all special programs and events. At the request of the Department one television station produced a commercial, dubbed it for the other area stations and ran it as a public service announcement (PSA). This first commercial was relatively simple, depicting the Department's programs in a comprehensive manner. The slogan was "Parks and Rec., more than you expect." The intent of this first effort was to inform and educate the public regarding the changes taking place in the Department. The Department continues to run PSAs especially focused on free, unsponsored programs and places (e.g., youth programs, parks, open spaces). The Department relies on paid television and newspaper advertising for major events (e.g., Brazos Nights). However, the majority of print advertising, posters, and other special event materials are printed for free by Waco's major newspaper, the *Tribune Herald*. The paper constantly promotes improvements to the parks and publishes pictures of facilities whenever possible. Department staff became regular guests on local television programs (e.g., Live at Five, Evening News, morning talk shows). In addition, staff members teach classes at Baylor University and hold presentations for civic groups such as Rotary, Kiwanis, the Parent-Teacher Associations and Chamber of Commerce.

Artwork is also capitalized on to promote Department programming although no artists exist in the Department's staff. The artwork for most programs is produced by Baylor University, McLennan Community College or Texas State Technical College in their graphic art departments as a part of class projects. Specialty brochures are prepared for area schools for STAR (Start the Afternoon with Recreation) and other park facilities such as First Street Cemetery and Miss Nellie's Pretty Place.

VIII. Impact of Change on the Agency

The change process left the Department staff with a legacy of increased professionalism. In addition to educational requirements for all new full-time employees, the Department mandates a minimum of 25 hours of annual training for current employees. Ongoing training must occur in at least three topic areas. The staff members' Texas Recreation and Parks Society dues are now paid by the Department. The staff members developed a greater appreciation for the value of leisure services through the implementation of their pricing systems at the facilities. The change process also generated more cooperation between the various divisions within the Department. For example, the Recreation Division now works with the Convention Center to plan and develop children's and spouses' programs associated with conventions. Recreation staff are beginning to understand Park-staff related problems and vice versa. The work force increased through contract personnel. The staff explored new techniques and methods to provide programs and maintain facilities. Restructuring allowed the staff to become more creative and, therefore, less stagnant in their thinking. Many employees are enjoying their jobs more and having more fun.

Two new program units—Athletics, and Special Events—were developed since 1989. Programs planned by these two units generated tourism revenues over $1.5 million dollars in 1993. With the establishment of its Performance Fund, the Department increased revenues from nothing in 1989, to just under $100,000 in the first year (1990) to more than $300,000 in the third year (1992). In addition, the grant and sponsorship sources acquired another $300,000-500,000 annually for the budget. Grants were obtained through agencies serving at-risk populations such as the PEW Partnership for Civic Change, the justice system and other area foundations. State-funded programs, such as the Summer Lunch Program and Texas Commission on the Arts, are also supporters of Department activities. The staff seeks sponsorships for major events through area businesses. All major special events must be underwritten by sponsors because they are free to the public. The following businesses supported Departmental programs in the past few years: NationsBank, Chrysler Technologies, HEB grocery stores, Dr. Pepper, Sprint Cellular, Central Texas Ford Dealers, Miller and Budweiser Distributing companies. Two cities, Bellmead and Woodway, also supported the Department.

IX. Impact of Change on the Community

A growing awareness of recreation division services, along with increasing participation in programs and park use, reflects the increased variety of classes offered, rising registration and expanding hours of operation to accommodate the public.

Community leaders, companies and agencies are increasingly requesting Recreation Division services. When moneys become available the Department sought to develop those programs. For example, 100 percent of 1993 Community Development Block Grant moneys were allocated to the Recreation Division for program development purposes. Adjacent school districts and cities are requesting the Department's assistance in establishing programs.

New services are added annually. Softball and tennis programs serve as the catalysts to build a new athletic complex—the second new facility built in the past ten years (the first being the new zoo).

In 1992, the Leisure Services Department and the Convention and Visitors Bureau merged into one department. The Convention Director was released, and the divisions within Leisure Services expanded. This change was implemented based on the programs, services, and credibility the Leisure Services Department gained since 1989. Advantages acquired from this arrangement include access to shared technology and equipment, better coordination of tournaments and conventions, and shared facilities for special events such as Brazos Nights.

X. Measurement of the Outcome

The intent of the Department was to measure outcomes four ways. First, program surveys conducted with participants determined their views and suggestions. The intent is to develop ongoing evaluation and avoid the inward, inactive focus that characterized Department operations prior to 1989. Nearly all of the Department's summer programs are now monitored annually and program surveys are expanding to other seasons on a random basis. Typically, the Department collects questionnaires on-site. In some cases, survey participants are rewarded. For example, Brazos Nights respondents are given free coupons for use at the events.

Second, attendance figures for all programs and events are monitored. Increased use and participation is evident in numerous venues from 1991 to 1993. Recreation center attendance increased from 5,000 to 20,000 annually; the Learn to Swim program participation rose from 400 to 800; the Fun in the Sun summer program attendance increased from 300 to 975; and facility rentals rose from 819 to 2,285. In its second year of operation (1993), Zoo attendance tripled its figures between July and December.

Third, tracking of the program-generated revenues and events provides an additional measure of accountability. The 1993 performance fund listed revenues of $308,720 which accrued from the following sources:

Softball	$233,820
Learn to Swim	28,500
Other Classes	15,000
Boat Tours	11,000
Special Events	11,000
Birthday Parties	9,400

Revenue tracking is not limited to internal sources since many of the Department-sponsored programs affected other businesses. Occupancy rates and food sales at area businesses are also monitored to determine economic spin-off effects of Departmental events [see Yardley, MacDonald and Clarke (1988) for an example of how these spin-off effects can be measured]. The Department also received a $3 million grant to expand the City's riverwalk system, and actively cooperated with other City agencies on grant request proposals.

Finally, budget increases provided by the City confirms value in the success of this change model. General Fund support of the Departmental operating budget increased from $579,500 in 1989 to $863,541 in 1993. The Capital Improvement Projects budget, dormant since 1968, was reinstated in 1989-1990 at $400,000. It rose to $500,000 in 1990-1991 and 1991-1992, and was set at $365,000 for 1992-1993. The Department funded numerous ventures in the past four years: six new playground sites, major repairs to facilities, new equipment for facilities, new programs for at-risk youth, a Counselor-in-training program, an expanded parks interpretive program, and additional full-time staff for recreation centers.

Author's Suggested Readings and References

Crompton, J. L. (1987). *Doing more with less in the delivery of recreation and park services: A book of case studies.* State College, PA: Venture Publishing, Inc.

Walsh, R. G. (1986). *Recreation economic decisions: Comparing benefits and costs.* State College, PA: Venture Publishing, Inc.

Yardley, J. K., MacDonald, J. H., & Clarke, B. D. (1988). The economic impact of a small, short-term recreation event on a local economy. *Journal of Park and Recreation Administration, 8*(4), pp. 71-83.

Sociodemographic Characteristics—

Arlington Heights

Arlington Heights, Illinois

1990 Population:
75,460

Median Age:
35.6

Household Composition:
85.1% in families

Chapter 12

Delegation of Authority: Arlington Heights Park District

Arlington Heights, Illinois

Gerald M. Oakes
Executive Director
Arlington Heights Park District

I. The Situation

Arlington Heights is Chicago's largest Cook County suburb. It is an upper middle class, highly educated, predominantly (98 percent) white community. Consistent with the Illinois system, the Arlington Heights Park District exists separate from city government, with its own taxation powers, and under the supervision of a five-member elected Park Board. In 1980 the Board of Commissioners voted unanimously to change the District's management from a centralized administrative structure to a decentralized system that maximized the skills and ability of the staff, emphasized customer service, and created a positive public image for the Park District.

Both the community and the District grew steadily in the past several decades. In 1980 the Park District employed 67 full-time and 400 part-time employees in four departments: parks, recreation, revenue facilities, and finance and personnel. The District assembled a talented professional staff, but many of their skills were underutilized due to the centralized nature of operations which were relatively effective when the District and the community it served were smaller. Relations were also strained between the Board and the Director. At the request of the Board, a management study was completed by a Chicago firm, Booze, Allen, & Hamilton, which outlined recommended changes needed to meet the Board's goals. Upon approval of the study's recommendations and after limited implementation of the proposals, the Executive Director was terminated by the Board. In February 1981 the Board hired a new Director of Parks and Recreation to implement the recommendations of the study.

The consultant's report identified three major problems. First, centralized decision making by the Director slowed attempts involving change and innovation and, therefore, underutilized the skills of the remainder of the staff. For example, existing procedures required that all District purchases be approved by the Director, and thus limited staff autonomy and hindered creativity. Second, the bureaucratic structure interfered with customer service and hindered the decision-making process. Under the old system supervisory staff had to clear even minor policy decisions with the Director, and registration for District programs was only available at one location in the community. Third, the District suffered from a loss of positive public image due to the problems related to administrative decision making. The media aired many of the District's internal problems during the late 1970s and early 1980s. The Board and Staff lacked a unified representative voice.

II. Vision

Change advocates envisioned a decentralized agency that would distribute decision-making responsibilities as much as possible throughout the staff, and, whenever possible, allow front-line staff to make final decisions. This policy applied to all departments within the agency.

III. Objectives

The Board of Commissioners developed five objectives:

1. To improve the Board/Staff relationship,

2. To enhance staff self-esteem,

3. To improve customer service,

4. To increase staff productivity, and

5. To raise the agency's image in both the community of Arlington Heights and in the State of Illinois.

IV. Management Paradigm Shift

To change the practice that all decisions had to be made by the Board or Director to a structure that not only encouraged, but demanded that line supervisors and front line employees solve problems and make decisions.

V. Key Players

Five elected Park board members, the Director of Parks and Recreation, four superintendents (representing each of the District's four departments), and 21 supervisors.

VI. Processes Undertaken to Accomplish Change

Once the policy change was approved in 1980, an interim plan was developed and implemented in 1981 to advise the Board and superintendents about the immediate action required to begin the decentralization process. This plan was in effect for approximately one year. Using staff input a long-range comprehensive plan was developed to lay out the direction the agency would take during the next five-year period. Once completed, it replaced the interim plan developed earlier in the year. Every third year the long-range plan is revised; the District is now using the fifth edition of the plan to guide its long-term policy.

Major components of the new policy—including public and community relations, and decentralization of supervisory authority—were implemented as soon as possible. Others, such as front-line staff decision-making powers, were phased in gradually. One reason for phasing in decision-making authority for front-line staff was to give the District time to develop reasonable standards and guidelines by which to make solid decisions. Each of the District's four departments developed its own set of recommendations for policies and procedures. The Director reviewed these policy recommendations which were then sent to and approved by the Board to ensure an adequate level of District-wide uniformity. By these means individual staff were given authority to make decisions as needed as long as they conformed with the established policies and procedures.

Decentralization. The Parks Department and the Recreation Department found the transition to decentralization the easiest. Both of these departments relied on large numbers of employees who were spread over the village and often worked odd-hour shifts. The finance, personnel, and revenue facilities divisions found the transition more difficult since they operated under different circumstances from those of their colleagues in parks and recreation. One extra hurdle the finance and personnel department faced was that they were undergoing a transition to computerize operations at the same time the decentralization policy was implemented.

For the first time in District history, four superintendents oversaw hiring authority for all full-time employees. In addition, purchasing authority was given to superintendents (up to $2,000 per purchase) and the Director (up to $10,000 per purchase) which was free from involvement by the Board of Commissioners.

With increased authority came additional responsibility. Therefore, it was important to provide adequate training to carry out expanded responsibilities and to develop reward structures appropriate to enhance acceptance of the new policy. Perhaps the most obvious intended rewards were intrinsic because the policy change allowed for greater autonomy and creativity among District employees. After adoption of the new policy, a series of workshops and training sessions were held to educate staff in decision making and to pass on the management philosophy of the agency. Both in-house and external consultants conducted these sessions. The District also provided funds to allow employees to attend state and national conferences and workshops. Perhaps the most important difference in the District's policy from those of other agencies is the number and scope of employees involved. For example, twenty District employees attended a recent trends workshop in Chicago in contrast to two or three top level supervisors as is common within most agencies.

It is important for employees to be confident that their decisions will be respected. Under a decentralized system, the Director must have a broader interpretation and tolerance for what is considered a success or failure than when operating in an authoritative system. Isolated failures and problems are tolerated as much as possible. Failure of a new program idea is not a problem in the Arlington Heights District. Since the implementation of the decentralized policy, many new ideas were tried. Some were successful; others failed. However, failure to adequately plan or follow-through with projects is problematic. A progressive discipline procedure deals with repeated mistakes of this nature. For example, failure to meet major deadlines would result in an employee receiving a written warning; three written warnings constitute grounds for dismissal.

Extrinsic rewards were also considered. The Park district enacted updated salary schedules to retain good staff and help to recruit new staff. Prior to 1981 the District's unwritten policy underpaid lower level supervisory staff so that they would leave after a couple of years with the agency. The new policy established a salary range with the intent to retain staff for longer periods of time. The widespread availability of professional development opportunities (already described) also provides extrinsic reward for staff members.

Community Relations. The District established a customer satisfaction guarantee program to set a high standard for customer service. Although practiced for several years on an informal basis, the satisfaction guaranteed program formalized in 1991. The policy is printed in the District's program brochure. Both the supervisors and desk staff have the authority to give refunds and resolve issues that inconvenience customers.

One example of the District's attempt to improve community relations involved the area of program registration procedures. Program registration decentralized from one central site to twelve locations in the community. In addition, registration procedures were computerized in order to ensure accuracy and speed the registration process. An employee recognition program was also established to recognize staff contributions to the agency.

VII. Marketing to Internal and/or External Publics

The Department took several steps to better ensure the success of the policy. Regular staff meetings are required for all departments in order to improve communication at all levels of operation. A newsletter that the Department started emphasizes employee recognition and staff accomplishments. This newsletter is distributed internally twelve times a year. Implemented training programs instilled confidence in staff and ensured that participants received consistent, reliable service in all programs. These policies help generate positive feelings among agency staff—and enhance the community's perception of the agency and its programs. These policies also reversed the public infighting that surfaced in the local media prior to the policy change.

External communication efforts about the District's policies and accomplishments are publicized in several ways. Employees are publicly recognized at Board meetings for their accomplishments. Likewise, the Director monitors the interests and involvement of individual Board members and gives public credit for successful ventures in those areas. Press releases on staff are continually being written for the local newspaper as background for articles and features. Members of the media are given background information on District activities, inquiries are handled promptly, and personal contact between District staff and media personnel is used to promote positive feelings about the Park District. In addition, an agency program brochure containing articles about staff and their accomplishments is published five times a year and direct-mailed to the community. The Department tried many different methods of communicating with residents and participants, but the direct-mail brochure with a consistent format and preannounced delivery time proved most effective in generating high program registration figures.

VIII. Impact of Change on the Agency

Line supervisors, with review by their immediate superior, hire their own full-time staff. This new policy allows supervisors to build their own teams without being dictated to by the Director. Experienced staff were recruited and continue to be retained because of the participatory management practices established by the Department. Staff professionalism is emphasized under the new system. College degrees and/or proven expertise is required for all new hires. Many employees have been with the District for all twelve years that the policy has been in effect, and their productivity and creativity levels continue to rise. The agency's Board is highly supportive of staff.

The number of recreation program offerings rose dramatically and consistently from the 1,444 offered in 1981, to 1,679 (1985), to 2,205 (1990), and to 2,581 in 1993 with only a 50 percent increase in full-time staff during the same time period. Parks facilities and grounds are in excellent condition even though the amount of maintained acreage increased by about 30 percent from 450 to 689 acres and staff increases were only minimal. Revenue facility participation and income is at an all time high.

The following points summarize the District's management philosophy. Management practices the belief that all work is valuable and important to the agency. Employees and Board members are recognized as having knowledge and skills that can make the agency even better, and they are given public credit for their accomplishments whenever possible.

IX. Impact of Change on the Community

Management's decisions are made in a timely manner, reducing the amount of bureaucratic red tape. For example, front-line facility staff are authorized to give on the spot refunds to dissatisfied participants. Likewise, high-quality parks exist because repairs are undertaken in a timely and efficient manner given the autonomy afforded to maintenance staff.

Participants have direct interaction and input with staff who make programming decisions. For example, the District's direct-mail brochure solicits comments from residents. Questions posed in each brochure average 300 open-ended responses allowing for input from approximately 1,500 respondents annually. Because the brochure is distributed to all community residents, this form of survey solicits opinions from both participants and nonparticipants. Nonparticipants are often ignored in survey research. In addition, participant surveys are conducted on a regular basis by sending postcard questionnaires to randomly selected program participants.

In summary, the agency is highly regarded in the community and thought to be a true asset which enriches the lives of Arlington Heights' residents.

X. Measurement of the Outcome

Numerous examples of external recognition reflect the success of the new operating policies. The agency won two National Park and Recreation Association (NRPA) Gold Medal Awards (1983, 1992). It received the Government Finance Officers' Association (GFOA) Certificate for Excellence in financial accounting six times; two national awards from the United States Tennis Association for outstanding facilities, and one Midwest Section award for Excellence in Tennis Programming.

The Illinois Parks and Recreation Association Distinguished Agency Certificate Program selected the Arlington Heights Park District as the test agency for its certification program; it received a total score of 94.4 on a 100 point scale. At this point there is no standard average to measure the score against because Arlington Heights is the first agency to be tested. However, the score represents competencies in the area of administrative practices, financial procedures, recreation programming, park operations, and revenue facility management.

Section Three: Neighborhood-Based Programs

Anaheim, California; Austin, Texas; Denver, Colorado; and Des Moines, Iowa, are large and important metropolitan areas that are easily recognizable to most Americans as centers of commerce, culture, and recreation. However, their high profiles do not make them immune from social and economic challenges that face all communities to some extent. All four of these cities developed pilot projects designed to improve conditions in their inner-city neighborhoods.

Like the cases presented in the two previous sections of this book, the four cases in this section are characterized by strong interagency cooperation. But the hallmark characteristic of the neighborhood-based programs was the speed at which they were implemented. Past neighborhood revitalization efforts, characterized by slow-moving, bureaucratic processes, frustrated both residents and administrators alike. However, these cases document four efforts where, after problems were identified, agencies sought to gain immediate footholds and credibility before building permanent relationships and facilities.

Sociodemographic Characteristics—

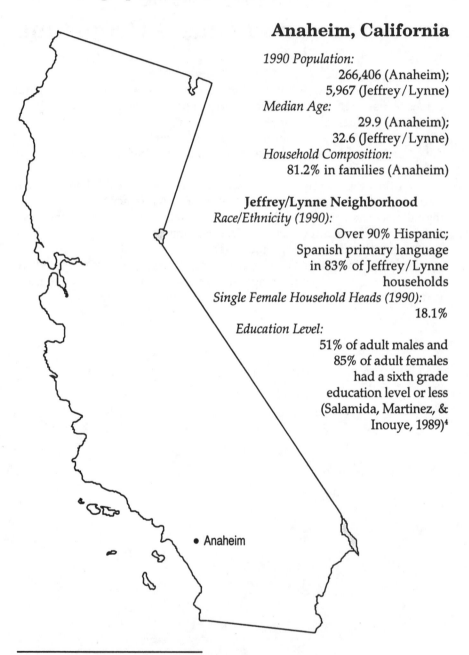

Anaheim, California

1990 Population:
266,406 (Anaheim);
5,967 (Jeffrey/Lynne)
Median Age:
29.9 (Anaheim);
32.6 (Jeffrey/Lynne)
Household Composition:
81.2% in families (Anaheim)

Jeffrey/Lynne Neighborhood
Race/Ethnicity (1990):
Over 90% Hispanic;
Spanish primary language
in 83% of Jeffrey/Lynne
households
Single Female Household Heads (1990):
18.1%
Education Level:
51% of adult males and
85% of adult females
had a sixth grade
education level or less
(Salamida, Martinez, &
Inouye, 1989)[4]

• Anaheim

---

[4]All other sociodemographic figures taken from the 1990 U.S. Census.

Chapter 13

Neighborhood Revitalization

Anaheim, California

Mark Deven
Recreation/Community Services Superintendent
Anaheim Department of Parks, Recreation and Community
Services

I. The Situation

The City of Anaheim has a number of neighborhoods that are characterized by overcrowding, high crime, sanitation problems, landlords who defer maintenance on their rental properties, illegal street vendors, and parking problems. The Jeffrey/Lynne neighborhood was identified as one of these areas.

The problems within Jeffrey/Lynne proved extremely complex and impossible to solve by functional, single-purpose service delivery systems associated with traditional forms of government. From the perspective of its residents, the City of Anaheim was not doing enough to make these areas more livable. From the perspective of city departments, these areas required far greater effort to manage than did the remainder of the City. Historically, Jeffrey/Lynne required above average outlays for police protection, code enforcement, street maintenance, and social services compared to other Anaheim neighborhoods. For the most part, the City departments impacted by the challenges were hard pressed to secure financial resources to deal with these neighborhoods on a selective basis.

In response to the public concerns about the neighborhood, the Anaheim City Council funded a human needs assessment in the area to determine the best methods for improving the overall quality of life. An additional challenge was to assist residents in addressing their concerns without changing the demographic composition of the community. Many Jeffrey/Lynne residents work in convention and visitor-related jobs which are of vital importance to the city's economy. The Jeffrey/Lynne neighborhood is located near many of Anaheim's tourism-related facilities and attractions. As such, it was important that proposed neighborhood improvements would not gentrify the neighborhood and displace current residents. This type of unanticipated spin-off occurred in an earlier project around Anaheim's Patrick Henry neighborhood following a major publicly and privately supported urban renewal effort.

Orange County Community Consortium, Inc. conducted the need assessment and produced a comprehensive document based on the available secondary data and 100 in-depth interviews with members of randomly selected Jeffrey/Lynne residents. At the conclusion of the study, the Consortium determined that there was a need for "an increase in communication in order to establish a link between the neighborhood and existing service providers." The study also identified the following ten specific human needs for residents of the neighborhood:

1. Implemented drug enforcement programs in Jeffrey/Lynne neighborhood;

2. Increased police visibility, enforcement, and involvement in the Jeffrey/Lynne community;

3. Community education;

4. Healthcare services (including insurance benefits);

5. Bilingual services;

6. English as a Second Language (ESL) classes;

7. Amnesty services;

8. Youth recreation;

9. Youth employment; and

10. Childcare for working parents.

The Consortium recommended that a mini-community center be established to serve the five block area, to facilitate communication between the various agencies and neighborhood residents, and to address the identified human needs.

II. Vision

The city envisioned the development of citizen involvement which would empower residents and landlords to work together to solve continuous and long-term problems. To do this, the city recognized the need to establish a small neighborhood park and minicommunity center that would provide residents with access to coordinated and integrated government services. The City would act as a direct service provider in some cases, and facilitate private involvement in other cases. For example, the City does not provide health insurance to residents but it does act as a facilitator between residents seeking insurance and the private companies that provide coverage.

III. Objectives

The Consortium developed six objectives:

1. To reduce incidents of crime and increase police presence in the area;

2. To reduce code enforcement violations stemming from deteriorating property and overcrowding;

3. To establish a temporary neighborhood center which would allow residents to access social services; and to replace the temporary center with permanent quarters as soon as possible (within two years);

4. To provide a permanent site for youth to access recreation programs;

5. To facilitate citizen participation in the development of solutions to neighborhood problems; and

6. To develop better cooperation between landlords and tenants to solve neighborhood problems.

IV. Management Paradigm Shift

For the first time ever, the City of Anaheim decided to cooperatively integrate law enforcement, code enforcement, human services and recreation into a coordinated service delivery system in a way that is issue-oriented, citizen-based, proactive, long-range, creative, and multidisciplinary.

V. Key Players

A Task Force formed with representatives (amount in parentheses) from the following departments of Anaheim's city government: City Manager's office (1); City Attorney (1); Community Development (1); Public Works / Engineering (1); Fire (1); Maintenance (1); Planning (two members, the Planning Director and the Code Enforcement Manager), Police (3); Parks, Recreation and Community Services (3); and Public Utilities (1). The Parks, Recreation and Community Services Director chaired the Task Force. Most of the committee members were Heads of their Departments. In most cases, membership was voluntary although selected members were assigned to the project in order to take advantages of special skills.

VI. Processes Undertaken to Accomplish Change

Initially, the Task Force believed that a concerted effort needed to be expended in the law and code enforcement areas to gain a "beachhead" before human services and recreation programs could be successfully introduced. The following paragraphs summarize the processes used to revitalize the Jeffrey/Lynne neighborhood which began in November 1989.

Code Enforcement. The consortium expended an extensive number of work hours in the Jeffrey/Lynne area dealing with code violations relating to housing, health and safety, parking, and street vendors. During the first three months of the program this effort revealed numerous substandard housing and public nuisance violations which resulted in two formal criminal complaints. The most common code violations included overcrowded houses and apartments, people living illegally in unconverted garages, cars parked on lawns, abandoned and stripped cars in the streets, and landlords who refused to repair damaged apartments.

After gaining the confidence of the tenants and the attention of the landlords, Code Enforcement's role switched to facilitative efforts that emphasized cooperation between a tenants' association and an apartment owners/managers group. Code Enforcement also produced special events to emphasize that they could do good things for the residents. These events were designed to build trust within the neighborhood. For example, they sponsor an annual neighborhood Christmas Fair with the Department of Parks, Recreation and Community Services, the Fire Department, and the Kiwanis Club.

Policing. The Consortium developed the Community-Based Policing program to address problems of crime in the area. This effort involved the temporary assignment of an officer who lived in the neighborhood and patrolled on foot, made numerous arrests, and established personal contact with law abiding citizens and children. After initial resistance, the Police Department facilitated the establishment of Neighborhood Watch units in the area. Many residents had a natural distrust for uniformed officers—some based on personal experiences with corrupt South and Central American police systems. It took several years to firmly establish this relationship and to gain the trust of most neighborhood residents. Consequently, when grant-funding for the community-based program ended, and the officer was pulled from the neighborhood, many residents expressed regret at the program's departure. In addition to normal calls for service, the Police Department continues to serve the area through the Neighborhood Watch program and special units such as narcotics and the gang detail.

Street/Security Lighting. The Public Utilities Department improved street lighting in the area within the first six months of the neighborhood revitalization effort. Since then, the Code Enforcement Officer sparked interest among property owners to install outdoor security lighting on buildings in order to light courtyards, alleys and landscaped areas that could hide illegal activity. The Utilities Department provides the lights at no cost to residents. Payback is based on increased electrical use for the lights and will occur in approximately five years after installation.

Recreation Programs. The Parks, Recreation and Community Services Department began serving the neighborhood through weekly visits by two mobile recreation units (step vans). One van, dubbed Fun on Wheels, provided a variety of recreation and sports equipment, and board games. The second van, the Art Mobile, provided crafts-related activities. Weekly visits, one by each van on different days, would generally draw 200 or more children. Recreation staff reported that the vans had the same effect as ice cream wagons for drawing children into the streets. Three bilingual staff members accompanied each van. The staff assigned to the van units blocked a section of street with traffic control equipment and conducted games and art activities. With the opening of the new neighborhood park, the Consortium eliminated regularly scheduled, weekly programs run from the vans, thus freeing them to serve other neighborhoods with little public open space. The current recreation program in Jeffrey/Lynne is open five days per week and provides a wide range of activities. The program incorporates activities which raise participants' self-esteem, discourage drug/gang activity, and instill neighborhood pride.

Community Center Establishment. In November 1989, a rental apartment was secured as a mini-community center for Jeffrey/Lynne. A community services outreach worker staffed the apartment and provided bilingual assistance, social service advocacy, and information and referral services.

In July 1991, the City purchased an eight-unit apartment complex which they extensively remodeled to accommodate typical neighborhood center uses. With the improved facilities, the outreach worker now facilitates the delivery of additional human services such as English as Second Language (ESL) classes, nutrition classes and a children's meals program. These services are provided directly by a nonprofit agency, the County and the School District.

Gang Outreach. The Parks, Recreation and Community Services Department, provides gang outreach workers in the neighborhood who contact at-risk youth in danger of using drugs, joining or already involved in gangs, or dropping out of school. Gang outreach services are provided both in the neighborhood's Community Center and at nearby junior and senior high schools. The gang outreach worker's office is located at the neighborhood center.

Park Development. Prior to initiation of the Jeffrey/Lynne project, no city parkland existed in the neighborhood. Although the nearest park was only one-half mile away, two major barriers existed to Jeffrey/Lynne residents: a major city street ran between the neighborhood and the park; and Jeffrey/Lynne residents had to cross a largely Anglo neighborhood which proved an intimidating prospect for many potential young recreators. In 1990 the Task Force began to explore the concept of closing part of a major neighborhood street, Audre Drive, in order to accommodate a street park. The concept required close study by, and coordination with, several departments. In addition, the Parks, Recreation and Community Services Department formed a steering committee composed of residents from Jeffrey/Lynne and surrounding neighborhoods to develop support for the concept. Disneyland provided in-kind technical assistance for the design phase of the project.

Today, Audre Plaza Park consists of a 1.5 acre recreational area adjoining the neighborhood center. They developed it by closing Audre Drive and installing recreation equipment and landscaping on what was once the street. They permanently closed Audre Drive to traffic by installing concrete barricades, pipe gates, and container tree plantings at the ends of the neighboring streets and alleys adjoining Audre Drive. Audre Drive was then resurfaced with a slurry coat[5] and recreation equipment, including swings and a playstack with a slide, were installed. The Department painted various types of games (e.g., hopscotch, four square, an action trail featuring Disney cartoon characters) on the street. The park was dedicated in May 1991. Daily attendance averages nearly 1,500 people, a substantial number for a neighborhood community of approximately 6,000 residents. As noted earlier, mobile recreation vans still visit Jeffrey/Lynne on occasion, but mobile vans are more often assigned to other isolated neighborhoods that do not have easy access to permanent parks, recreation facilities and programs.

VII. Marketing to Internal and/or External Publics

The most important external marketing components went beyond promotion and included the comprehensive programming developed by the Jeffrey/Lynne task force and the innovative temporary and permanent distribution solutions that created facilities within reach of neighborhood residents. However, promotion efforts were also developed. A concerted effort informed both the electronic and print media of city efforts to revitalize Jeffrey/Lynne. Although both Spanish and English language print media picked up the story, television coverage appeared only in English. These efforts introduced the project to residents of surrounding neighborhoods as well as within Jeffrey/Lynne. During the past year, additional external marketing occurred within professional organizations which serve local government and the Department of Parks, Recreation and Community Services.

---

[5] A thin, smooth coat of asphalt. Rubberized surfaces were also installed under some play equipment.

Several internal promotion efforts were also initiated. The initial involvement of City Council included their participation in a study session on the project. The Council remained updated on the Jeffrey/Lynne project progress through general informational reports and staff reports related to specific actions. A City Council workshop which summarized the project's status was conducted prior to the completion of the street park. Department staff regularly informed the Community Services Board, and Park and Recreation Commission about the status of the project.

VIII. Impact of Change on the Agency

The success of the Jeffrey/Lynne project encouraged more interdepartmental cooperation. The departments involved in this project became focused on issues, citizen needs and long-term solutions, and became more proactive and creative. The project has, to some extent, enhanced the credibility and standing of the Department of Parks, Recreation and Community Services. This standing has already yielded political benefits. Despite budget reductions in many City services, programs which serve at-risk youth or meet critical human needs remained largely intact. In fact, another project which recently began in another distressed Anaheim neighborhood used the Jeffrey/Lynne model as a prototype. This project in the Avon/Dakota/Eton neighborhood involves an area which is similar to, but slightly smaller than Jeffrey/Lynne.

IX. Impact of Change on the Community

The most significant impacts of the project on the Jeffrey/Lynne neighborhood were the empowerment of its residents, and establishment of trust in city government. Residents actively participate in neighborhood affairs and volunteer for community projects such as street tree plantings and graffiti removal. Despite the normal distrust of government which is common to many immigrants from Latin America, the outreach workers, recreation staff, code enforcement and police officers who work the area are accepted and trusted by the residents.

X. Measurement of the Outcome

Measurement of the project will occur in two ways. First, the department plans to administer a users' survey to residents who frequent the neighborhood center. The Consortium developed survey instrumentation. The data, collected primarily with close-ended questions on a paper and pencil questionnaire, was collected in person by researchers similar to the method used in the initial Needs Assessment. A focus committee composed of neighborhood residents and apartment owners is presently discussing the survey results in order to develop a long-term action plan.

Second, the steering committee that was formed to evaluate the use of the street park will remain in place to monitor traffic, noise, parking, loitering, and security/street lighting issues. One potential problem that was anticipated, but did not develop, involved the increased traffic on adjacent streets caused by the closing of Audre Drive to create the street park. Each of the potential problems associated with the street park may be evaluated through periodic traffic counts, noise/nuisance complaints, and crime statistics. Most of these data are to be drawn from regular Police Department statistics.

External recognition has been limited to date because such recognition has not been sought. However, the Department of Parks, Recreation and Community Services applied for consideration for the Helen Putnam Award for Excellence in Government that is presented annually by the League of California Cities. In 1994 the Department received notification that it won the Grand Prize Award in the Community Services Partnership category. Also, the American Planning Association recognized the City of Anaheim in the past year with a state-level Advocacy Planning Award for the new efforts in the Avon/Dakota/Eton neighborhood.

Author's Suggested Readings and References

Salamida, M. A., Martinez, I., and Inouye, C. S. (1989). *Jeffrey-Lynne Project: 1988-1989 Needs Assessment.* Anaheim, CA: Orange County Community Consortium.

Sociodemographic Characteristics—

Austin, Texas

1990 Population:
          465,622 (Austin);
        10,864 (Dove Springs)
Median Age:
          28.9 (Austin);
        24.6 (Dove Springs)
Household Composition:
      69.7% in families (Austin);
    82.3% in families (Dove Springs)

Dove Springs Neighborhood

Race/Ethnicity:

1980	1990
24.4% Hispanic;	44.5% Hispanic;
62.9% White;	31.2% White;
9.7% Black	21.3% Black

Single Female Heads of Household:

1980	1990
7.3%	17.4%

Poverty Rate :

1980	1990
5.4%	22.0%

● Austin

Chapter 14

Self-Reliant Neighborhood

Austin, Texas

Robert Sopronyi
(former) Programs Division Manager
Austin Parks and Recreation Department

I. The Situation

Adolescents' experiences associated with growing up have undergone dramatic changes in the past several decades. Fundamental changes in the structure of American families strain the capacity of parents and guardians to provide young people with the care and guidance they need to cope with the challenges of daily life.

Austin, like many urban areas, is experiencing an increase in violent and disruptive youth behavior. Families, schools, and community organizations have been slow to adapt to new social circumstances. As a primary provider and facilitator of recreational opportunities for youth, the City of Austin Parks and Recreation Department attempted to meet this challenge by shifting its service commitment and delivery strategies. The Department adopted a facilitative role to coordinate service delivery efforts by multiple agencies. To paraphrase the advice of an African proverb: It takes a whole village to educate a child.

Traditional undifferentiated programming strategies are often inappropriate for diverse communities. Thus, rather than develop an untargeted comprehensive program for addressing neighborhood issues across the entire city, the Department identified a target community to begin providing multifunctional services.

Dove Springs, the selected target community, is a residential area that encompasses three census tracts (Austin Parks and Recreation Department, 1993). It is a lower-middle class, ethnically diverse neighborhood with a high percentage of families and the highest youth concentration of any neighborhood within the city limits. However, at the time of its selection for the pilot project, this vast residential neighborhood lacked public facilities with the exception of schools and little commercial development. Census statistics from 1980 and 1990 show that over half of the Anglo population left the area, while the Black and Hispanic populations increased 11.6 percent and 20.1 percent respectively. Home ownership declined by 27.9 percent during that same period. Approximately 17 percent of all rental property housed five or more individuals. The poverty rate increased by 16.6 percent from 1980 to 1990. Youth criminal activity was significant. Dove Springs comprised the majority of Austin's police sector which held the highest percent of gang-related crimes. Health concerns included a higher than average number of teen births, low birth weights, infant deaths, and reportable diseases.[6] There were no public clinics staffed with physicians in the three targeted census tracts comprising Dove Springs.

II. Vision

The Department's vision was to develop and maintain a service delivery process that included the entire community, had a long-term impact, and met a variety of service and developmental needs. The stated goal of the project was to provide City of Austin assistance to the Dove Springs Neighborhood through its leaders and service providers and to enable the community to become self-reliant within a twelve-month period.

III. Objectives

The Department developed three objectives:

1. To provide expanded recreational and social services to the (Dove Springs) target community.

2. To provide interim community services until a permanent facility is complete.

3. To build a permanent recreation center in Dove Springs Community by 1994.

IV. Management Paradigm Shift

The major paradigm shift involved transforming the Department of Parks and Recreation from a "bats and balls" organization into an "opportunity and personal growth" organization. In the case of this project, recreation activities were not only viewed simply as ends in themselves, but also as vehicles for

---

[6] A disease that is highly contagious and potentially life threatening but considered controllable, such as salmonella, tuberculosis, or AIDS (Mosby's Medical Dictionary, 3rd ed., 1989)

achieving broader outcomes including: development of self-esteem, decision-making skills, coping skills, and social skills among participants. Individuals in the Dove Springs community expressed concerns about the lack of services, the deterioration of the neighborhood, the school dropout rate, gang and criminal activity, and the lack of recreational/library facilities. For example, dropout rates at Johnston High, which serves the Dove Springs community, averaged fifteen to sixteen percent annually in the early 1990s as compared to the Austin average of about nine percent. The community's Mendez Middle School noted dropout rates of three to four percent during this time period (most middle school students are young enough that, by law, they must remain in school). The City reviewed some of the basic necessities and determined that a multipurpose center could best suit the needs of this vast, yet isolated, inner-city community.

Consistent with its pump-priming objectives and facilitative approach, the City planned to divest itself of as many social/parenting services as possible within a twelve-month period. By that time, it was hoped that the neighborhood groups and individual leaders would take the responsibility and instill these leadership ideals in their community. Indeed, temporary services were in place by 1993, and most city officials responsible for strategic planning and program information (e.g., the City Manager's Office) turned over responsibility to the neighborhood on June 1, 1994. The City presence will remain, both technically and philosophically, in the form of the recreation center, library, and police store front.

V. Key Players

A large, comprehensive group of private organizations, city agencies and individuals spearheaded the Dove Springs effort: four representatives from the Parks and Recreation Department; two representatives from the Library Department; two representatives from the Health and Human Services Department; a representative from the Police Department; a representative from the Boys and Girls Club; the Assistant City Manager; Dove Springs Advisory Board; Austin City Council; Parks Board; and the Austin Independent School District.

VI. Processes Undertaken to Accomplish Change

Several Dove Springs organizations inquired about solving neighborhood problems and sought assistance from the Department of Parks and Recreation in 1992. As a group, existing neighborhood organizations provided the Department with data and ongoing information on residents' programming needs. One of the most interesting components about residents' concerns for their neighborhood was the lack of recreational facilities and programs. They also indicated a preference for receiving additional recreational services prior to receiving the other needed services. With this understanding, Parks and Recreation staff members determined that the Department could not turn the community around alone. After a lease was approved for a temporary recreation center site, Police Store front, and the Health Department's Women's Infant and Children (WIC) Program, Recreation staff decided that the temporary recreation center would include space for a small library, homework center, and drug and dropout counseling. The center can also be used for community groups to hold meetings. Other city services using the multipurpose center were encouraged to make themselves visible in the temporary recreation center. In addition, the Boys/Girls Club of Austin was brought in, not only for their expertise, but also because they offered recreational equipment and assistance in staffing the operation. The center will act as a catalyst to provide information for the community regarding jobs, dropout/drug counseling, health services, and parenting classes.

A city-wide Capital Improvements referendum held in May 1992 included a request for funds to finance a recreation center and library for the Dove Springs area. Voters approved the bonds to construct a recreation center and branch library in Dove Springs. In October 1992, the recreation center bonds were sold. Construction of the facility began in September 1994. Once completed, the facility will serve as the centerpiece of the City's efforts to provide permanent recreation services for Dove Springs. The adjacent park and pool facilities opened in June 1994.

Residents, more than willing to participate in the revitalization of their community, lacked assistance from the City to help in the coordination of essential services, and required assistance to bring the leaders together into one organization. By including a variety of agencies in the planning process, the Parks and Recreation Department began consolidation of services and offered the community the level of programs necessary to meet their vision.

Residents in the Dove Springs community, concerned that conditions would continue to deteriorate until the completion of the recreation facility, asked community leaders to approach the City to provide interim services. These leaders asked City staff to investigate possibilities about leasing the only vacant building in the Dove Springs community large enough to serve as a recreation center until the permanent center is built.

The Parks Board approved the lease concept of the vacant building, a former Walgreen's store, located at a prominent major intersection. City Council approved a budget amendment in February 1993 to lease the building and began to offer services in May 1993. Originally, the Dove Springs Neighborhood Association was to acquire the site and turn it over to the Parks and Recreation Department so it could begin to provide services. However, the Department ended up assuming responsibility for site acquisition because the Dove Springs Neighborhood Association could not generate enough money to lease a facility of the necessary scale on such short notice. The Department's sufficient financial and organizational resources allowed it to make the immediate commitment. Departmental staff accepted the challenge; they were serious about the partnership, and they wanted to initiate the project before the momentum was lost.

VII. Marketing to Internal and/or External Publics

Most early marketing efforts were internal since the intent of the project was to develop a solid working relationship between the Department and the Neighborhood Association. Therefore, concerted efforts focused on the cultivation of trust and understanding, so the Department sought to limit external marketing efforts in the initial stages of the project. They expected that the Neighborhood Association and Dove Springs residents would become catalysts for external marketing efforts once the project was established.

The first external marketing efforts occurred in May of 1993 with anticipation of the temporary community center. The most visible promotion effort involved a major media event that drew politicians and other dignitaries to the center. Promotion was deemphasized in the marketing mix because of extensive attention to other components such as the previously described program development and distribution concerns. Most program suggestions originated from the potential participants and were brought to the Dove Springs Advisory Board by representatives of community groups. This attention to program and distribution strategies minimized most of the need for educational and persuasive promotion efforts. The location of the community center within the Dove Springs neighborhood represented a major distribution-related advance because no services existed there previously. Efforts were made to form a staff with a similar racial and ethnic balance to the Dove Springs neighborhood. Consistent with Austin Department of Parks and Recreation policy, all written promotional literature for the Dove Springs project is printed in both English and Spanish.

VIII. Impact of Change on the Agency

The Parks and Recreation Department began to appeal and respond to the diverse needs and interests of the Austin community. Its approach differed from the traditional distribution paradigm which attempted to deliver services *equally* across *all* sections of the community. Although the traditional paradigm had intuitive appeal, it is often ineffective due to potential participants bringing unique experiences and circumstances with them. The new paradigm represents a shift from the traditional "equal opportunity equity model" to a "compensatory equity model" whereby disadvantaged groups and areas receive special consideration. Indeed, independent research conducted in Austin in the past suggested that residents had stronger preferences for compensatory service delivery models than did many of the Parks and Recreation Department staff (Wicks & Crompton, 1987). The Department created a strong leadership committed to generating policies in order to reach underserved citizens in low-income, urban neighborhoods. Dove Springs served as the pilot neighborhood for this effort.

The Department began to reach out to families, schools, health services and a wide-variety of community partners who are committed to community development. This effort placed the Parks and Recreation Department in the larger community arena.

Rather than delivering a limited range of services in isolation from other agencies and groups, the Department is now a tangible part of a larger system. In addition to participating in the process, Parks and Recreation personnel assumed leadership roles by aiding in the coordination and facilitation efforts of other agencies.

IX. Impact of Change on the Community

As one of the first major decentralized, collaborative service delivery efforts attempted by the City, the program is designed to help strengthen the diversity and quality of adult leadership to reflect the racial and ethnic composition of the community. In addition, it is proposed to enhance the role of young people and community leaders as resources in their own communities through their participation in community services and the design and operation of programs. City agencies plan to divest themselves as direct providers of some services as the community becomes increasingly self-sufficient. This will free City resources which can be concentrated in additional areas of great need.

X. Measurement of the Outcome

Measurement procedures are still developing. The Parks and Recreation Department will work with the Police Department, Youth Advocacy, Travis County Youth Services and Austin Independent School District. The agencies will design a model to measure:

1. The level of gang-related crimes in the community.

2. The level of teen pregnancies in the community.

3. Trends in school attendance at elementary, middle and high schools that serve the community.

4. The level of self-reliant development in the community.

Measurement of progress will occur on two levels—community-wide and individual. Auditors from the five agencies are currently developing community-wide, performance-based budgets and grids for the four variables listed previously. These measures will occur on a long-term basis as it is expected that a minimum tracking period of five years will be necessary for a realistic measurement of trends. A second project will track the progress of individual children and youth in the community. Results of these initiatives are published on a quarterly basis by the City Manager's Office under the title *Opportunities for Youth*. This March 1994 publication reported tangible progress on several fronts. For example, the Johnston High dropout rate decreased to less than five percent in the past year (Austin City Manager's Office, 1994).

Author's Suggested Readings and References

Austin Parks and Recreation Department. (1993). *Dove Springs Self-Reliant Neighborhood Project Report*. Austin, TX: Author.

Austin City Manager's Office. (1994, March). *Opportunities for Youth (second quarter)*. Austin, TX: Author.

Wicks, B. E., and Crompton, J. L. (1987). An analysis of the relationship between equity choice preferences, service type and decision-making groups in a U.S. city. *Journal of Leisure Research, 19*, pp. 189-204.

Sociodemographic Characteristics—

Denver, Colorado

1990 Population:

467,610

Median Age:

33.8 (Denver);
19% aged 5-17 (Five Points/Mestizo-Curtis Park);
21% aged 5-17 (Araria-Lincoln Park)

Household Composition:

69.9% in families (Denver);
55.9% in families (Five Points/Mestizo-Curtis Park);
60.7% in families (Araria-Lincoln Park)

▲ Denver

Five Points/Mestizo-Curtis Park Neighborhood

1990 Population:

8,065

Race/Ethnicity:

36.6% Black;
40.9% Hispanic;
19.6% White

Single Parent Families with Children:
22.6%

Araria-Lincoln Park Neighborhood

1990 Population:

6,591

Race/Ethnicity:

37.9% Black;
28.3% Hispanic;
27.8% White

Single Parent Families with Children:
22.7%

Chapter 15

Night Moves

Denver, Colorado

Theresa Rash
Operation Section Manager
Denver Parks and Recreation Department

I. The Situation

Residents of the Five Points/Mestizo-Curtis Park and the Araria-Lincoln Park neighborhoods are good, decent people who are victimized by the high crime rate and socioeconomic deprivation which sometimes occurs in urban cities. Their children are victims of the times who have been damaged by the demeaning first-hand experiences caused by physical violence and/or the mental abuse caused by the constant threat of being victimized within their community, at school, or in their own homes. These youths are subject to higher drop-out rates from a public school system in a nation which often appears to be indifferent to their needs. In some cases, these youths are victimized by parents who lose hope and tune-out their kids' lives, because they themselves have been tuned out by society.

II. Vision

The project targeted youth between twelve and seventeen years of age. These youth live in an environment where they are exposed to poverty, violence, abuse, gangs, illiteracy, indifference, and loneliness. The vision was to design a project which gives these youth positive and relevant recreational opportunities which would attract their interest—a project that would show them how better to utilize the available support systems; help them realize their maximum potential, develop higher opinions of themselves, and enjoy what is left of their childhood.

III. Objectives

The visionaries developed three objectives:

1. To provide Denver youth positive alternatives to skipping school, substance abuse, gang/negative behavior, and low self-esteem during late evening hours.

2. To develop collaborative efforts between the public and private sectors committed to provide overall hands-on administrative and financial support for the youth project.

3. To recruit a Youth Advisory Board charged with meeting on a regular basis to determine how and when the project will operate and what programs will be offered.

Members of the advisory board were recruited from Glenarm and LaAlma community centers (three representatives each), and from the Denver Housing Authority (three representatives). Membership of the Youth Advisory Board varies throughout the year. Members usually serve three-month terms.

IV. Management Paradigm Shift

The most important paradigm shift was to reschedule recreation employees (supervisors and field staff) who were accustomed to ending their workday by 6:00 or 8:00 p.m. to work shifts ending at 9:00 p.m. weekdays and between 10:00 p.m. and 12:00 midnight on Friday and Saturday nights—when the youth wanted to recreate. Essentially this represented a shift from an inward-oriented product approach to an outward-directed marketing approach.

A second paradigm shift was to develop close working relationships between the city agency (e.g., Parks and Recreation, Denver Housing Authority) and representatives from private business (e.g., Denver Nuggets). This strategy differs from the autonomous operating procedures common to most municipal leisure service delivery systems.

V. Key Players

The collaborative effort established included: the Mayor of Denver; the Denver Nuggets Community Fund; Denver Housing Authority; Five Points/ Mestizo-Curtis Park Community youth; Araria-Lincoln Park Community youth; the nine Youth Advisory Board members; the Glenarm Recreation Center staff; the LaAlma Recreation Center staff; the Deputy Manager for Recreation; and the Recreation Operation Section Manager who coordinated the project.

VI. Processes Undertaken to Accomplish Change

In late 1991 the Deputy Manager of Denver Recreation sought alternative ways to impact youth throughout Denver. The Operating Section Manager was assigned to researching ideas and identifying possible sites to pilot new approaches for offering youth leisure activities. Some consensus in the community stated that opportunities should be expanded. Citizen groups advocated for more late evening and weekend access to recreation centers.

Coincidentally, attendance at NBA-Denver Nuggets games was declining rapidly at that time. The new management team of the Nuggets felt that the franchise needed to become a positive force within the Denver community. The Nuggets organization made the initial contact with the Deputy Manager who recognized their inquiry as an opportunity to offer some exciting new opportunities for the city's youth.

After identifying interested Parks and Recreation staff members and sites, a series of meetings were coordinated with the Nuggets organization by the Deputy Manager who served as facilitator. As the group brainstormed ideas, it became apparent that a hook was needed to get disconnected youth involved in leisure activities; a hook which would help these boys and girls avoid the pitfalls that prevent them from getting an education. The hook was initially identified to be basketball. However, the more the group met and listened to what the youth were telling them, the more it became apparent that the young people knew what they wanted and needed.

It was not just sports. Other recreational activities such as horseback riding and education opportunities such as computer literacy classes became part of the program. Their vision was wide, encompassing a variety of educational and social goals. However, the youth did not know how to acquire the experiences and skills they desired.

After several discussions with youth representatives to obtain input, a pilot project was created. This pilot consisted of three components. The first component would provide recreational and competitive program opportunities for middle school and high school aged boys and girls on Friday and Saturday nights between 6:00 and 10:00 p.m. The second component would provide educational enrichment opportunities to be offered two or three evenings per week after school. Both components incorporated an escort/security system consisting of male and female security guards to maximize both female and male participation during late-evening and after-dark hours. The third component promoted the Night Moves project and educated audiences about the variety of programs available.

The project title "Night Moves" was adopted during one of the early meetings. It was also decided that an active Youth Advisory Board should determine how the Night Moves project should look. The Operating Section Manager prepared a tentative design of the project which incorporated the ideas received from the young, but wise, participants. Staff members raised the issue of extrinsic incentives. The program staff designed a four-tiered incentive requirement program. In order to receive the maximum number of incentives the youth are required (1) to attend a designated number of recreation activities; (2) to attend a designated number of enrichment sessions/workshops/clinics; (3) to present school progress reports/report cards as requested by Night Moves staff; and, (4) each youth would be required to participate in three activities with at least one parent/adult during the term of the project. All requirements, incentives, and disciplinary actions are to have input by the Youth Advisory Board.

As plans progressed, the Denver Housing Authority (DHA) was seeking to address the growing numbers of idle youth living in their units. They obtained the financial resources, but lacked physical resources suitable for recreation programming and expertise to address the youths' recreational needs. However, DHA became aware of the negotiations between the Denver Recreation Department and Denver Nuggets to provide recreation opportunities for at-risk youth. After several telephone conversations with the Deputy Manager, a meeting was held with DHA, the Nuggets and the Recreation Department administrative representatives to determine if each agency's needs and commitments were compatible. DHA, interested in establishing an NBA franchise program called Midnight Basketball, targeted young adults ages eighteen to twenty-five. However, because the youth targeted by the Night Moves program were twelve to seventeen years of age, and Denver's curfew regulations restrict late-night mobility of this age group, the Midnight Basketball design was not adopted or pursued at that point.

The groups agreed that their three agencies would co-sponsor the Night Moves project. These agencies also agreed that the initially identified sites would be changed to better serve the largest number of youth living in disadvantaged communities and public housing. From a list of eight possible sites under consideration, two were selected for the pilot project. Denver Parks and Recreation Departments' Glenarm Recreation Center which served the Five Points/Mestizo-Curtis Park communities, and LaAlma Recreation Center which served the Araria-Lincoln Park communities were selected as initial project sites. Since private money was used to fund the pilot project, the site selection committee could afford greater control. If tax money was involved, there may have been greater pressure to spread the project over a larger area.

The key players met over a period of two months in a strategic planning process to establish working relationships between the Youth Advisory Board members and project sponsors. Early sessions focused on brainstorming for ideas and later sessions served to establish programmatic details. The committee created and prioritized project components, identified program incentives, reviewed the project time table, developed a first-year budget for each site, and developed public service announcements promoting Night Moves.

From February to May 1992, the implemented three-month pilot project included Friday and Saturday night basketball leagues and after-school education enrichment sessions including computer literacy. The second year of the project was funded in-part by an Urban Park and Recreation Recovery (UPARR) grant and support from the Robert R. McCormick Tribune Foundation which was obtained with strong backing from Denver's Mayor. The Nuggets sponsored the computer center at the Glenarm Center and a small local company, Whiz Bang, provided software and maintenance support.

VII. Marketing to Internal and/or External Publics

An annual membership fee of $1 provides an indication of the youths' interest in the program but does not screen out participants based on ability to pay. Promotional efforts were easily developed compared to the attention that had been given to other marketing mix components such as program development and distribution. The Denver Nuggets utilized their media resources to hold a press conference in November 1991 to create a public service announcement promoting the Night Moves registration dates. Flyers were distributed to outline program details. Following this initial attempt at informing potential participants, promotional efforts relied heavily on personal contact and celebrity appearances. Students from three high schools and two middle schools participated in television promotions at McNichols Arena with Nuggets player Marcus Liberty. The Harlem Globetrotters held several exhibition games with twenty-five cents from each ticket sold (totaling $1,200) going to the Night Moves project. Globetrotter star Curly Neal conducted a Stay-in-School basketball clinic at the Glenarm Recreation Center site in January 1992. The Nuggets sponsored other clinics.

Publicity efforts in the second year were also characterized by interagency and business cooperation. *The Denver Post* did a full-page article with color pictures on the Night Moves project in January 1993. Earvin Magic Johnson's Magic for Kids clinic held a fundraiser for a local cancer association featuring 60 Night Moves participants in clinic drills which was covered by both Denver newspapers and featured on all four major television stations. Johnson autographed basketballs for each Night Moves site in April 1993. Television stations, Channels Four and Two, continue to run public service announcements throughout the Denver area promoting Night Moves' upcoming events. Project site staff members regularly visit schools to promote Night Moves programs, and local stay-in-school efforts.

VIII. Impact of Change on the Agency

The Night Moves project generated a healthy competition to create bigger and better youth opportunities among the 21 other recreation centers operated by Denver's Parks and Recreation Department. This project challenges employees to change traditional approaches to recreation programming. The healthy competition gave program ingenuity and creativity a much needed boost. It also placed the Department in the dynamic center of a multiagency/business cooperative effort that underscores positive community benefits accruing from recreation and raised the public profile of the Department.

Night Moves is run by two paid Departmental staff members at each site, with an additional three or four on-call staff members as attendance warrants. The Department seeks paid staff for their interpersonal training and technical skills related to the recreational activity and educational activity mix at each site. Turnover among paid staff has been very low during the duration of the Night Moves project. In addition, each site benefits from the assistance of several volunteers. Both the Nuggets and the DHA provide volunteer lists. Volunteers are screened regarding their level of interest and commitment to the project by Departmental staff. They are then given a trial period on-site and retained if the kids warm-up to them and benefit from their presence.

IX. Impact of Change on the Community

The Night Moves design generated an increased number of volunteers willing to assist during prime-time hours at each site. Committed volunteers addressed the need for tutorial instructors which resulted in improved youth self-esteem, lower school absenteeism and improved grades. Increased facility access hours so parents and youth can interact in a leisure environment improved agency/community relations and parent-child communications. Having a safe place to be away from home fostered self-confidence in youth, reduced youth offenses, and improved neighborhood pride.

Expansion of Night Moves to two additional sites is projected for 1994. Denver was selected to host the 1994 Housing and Urban Development (HUD) National Basketball Tournament due to, in part, the success of the Night Moves Program.

X. Measurement of the Outcome

The outcome of the project is consistently monitored throughout the course of each year. The Night Moves incentive components require registration and nightly attendance rosters. Youth members must attend a minimum number of events in order to qualify for incentives such as horseback riding expeditions outside of town. Many participants who previously had little or no experiences outside the urban environment are now more appreciative and supportive of environmental conservation. Monthly school progress reports and report cards are collected and reviewed to identify strong/weak learning abilities. School report cards are posted publicly so participants can challenge and compete with each other. Project sponsors and the Youth Advisory Board will continue to meet regularly to review program needs, budget distribution, discipline problems, and incentives.

Sociodemographic Characteristics—

Des Moines, Iowa

1990 Population:

193,187

Median Age:

32.2

Household Composition:

76.2% in families

Downtown Core and Adjacent Neighborhoods[7]

Race/Ethnicity (1990):

63% White;
28% Black;
9% Other

Single Female Head of Households (1990):

37.9%

Poverty Rate (1990):

20% to 40% of households in each tract

---

[7] Includes census tracts 12, 17, 26, 27, 42, and 48-52.

Chapter 16

Downtown Recreation Opportunities for Youth

Des Moines, Iowa

Don Tripp
Director of Parks and Recreation

I. The Situation

Like many communities throughout the country, Des Moines periodically wrestled with the issue of providing positive recreational activities for its youth. Downtown Des Moines experienced a heavy increase in teenage "loop-scooping" activities beginning in 1990. Driving the strip is a popular activity, especially in many small towns. Generally, this activity is little more than an occasional annoyance when several dozen teens are involved. However, it became a problem in Des Moines since the downtown street layout includes several three-lane, one-way streets, and there is a relatively large population in the community. Renewed popularity of loop-scooping resulted in influxes of several thousand young adults on Friday and Saturday nights throughout the spring and summer.

These gatherings brought a general increase in crime to both property and persons. Fights became increasingly common and evidence of both gang involvement and weapons surfaced. Media coverage of the phenomenon became more sensational and intense due to a drive-by shooting. Downtown businesses, especially those that depended on evening crowds, suffered a feeling of insecurity in downtown Des Moines. Further, it was apparent that many of the youth were simply looking for something to do. The Des Moines Park and Recreation Department, concerned about the teenagers involved, offered to attempt to provide alternatives. This would not be easy.

At the same time loop-scooping and associated problems escalated, the City was reeling from cutbacks that diminished the effectiveness of neighborhood recreation facilities. Property taxes froze in 1990 and City government was more than $4 million over budget. The City's five community centers operated only 40 hours per each week (down from 100-hour weeks a decade earlier). Traditional delivery perspectives lacked sufficient resources to run quality programs in City community centers, swimming pools, and neighborhood parks. In sum, a clear need for more youth activities, both in neighborhoods and downtown, existed, but the diminishment of funds grossly affected recreation opportunities. In a long-term gamble to reverse the community's poor economic fortunes, property taxes on new developments were abated in 1988. Under this policy, new home owners paid no property taxes for five years. Although housing starts were increasing in the City, the positive benefits of the tax abatement policy were not yet being realized.

II. Vision

The Department's vision was to provide a highly-visible alternative for youth involved in downtown loop-scooping. Staff believed that their Department could offer a recreation alternative that teens would choose over simply "hanging out." There were no illusions that recreation programming could solve the problem, but they could serve as part of a long-term solution. Further, the Department believed that a collaborative effort could be built to allow for expanded services at neighborhood-based recreation facilities.

III. Objectives

Four objectives guided the effort:

1. Move teens from cars and the street to organized recreation activities.

2. Provide a program which was multicultural. Although racial tension was not a major problem, the residential neighborhoods adjacent to downtown were predominantly African-American and many of the loop-scoopers were white youth from other parts of the City, suburbs, and surrounding towns.

3. Expand teen services at neighborhood recreation centers.

4. Collaborate with other recreation providers (i.e., nonprofit and commercial) in the hope of building long-term, mutually beneficial relationships.

IV. Management Paradigm Shift

Two critical results were sought by responding to this recognized community issue: first, to show that the Des Moines Park and Recreation Department was capable of responding, on short notice, to special recreation needs; and second, to see if the Des Moines Park and Recreation Department could serve as a facilitator and collaborator instead of sole proprietary program manager.

The first issue was primarily attitudinal. Department staff were accustomed to working under stringent planning guidelines that fostered deliberate action. The second issue was also potentially volatile. Like most professionals, Department staff were reluctant to admit that they couldn't do it all and might require outside assistance to successfully tackle the problem.

V. Key Players

The coalition that evolved consisted of representatives from City Council, two city departments (Parks and Recreation and Police), two private nonprofit agencies (Metro YMCA and Urban Dreams, a minority youth serving agency), and the Milton Eisenhower Foundation.

VI. Processes Undertaken to Accomplish Change

The program began with a "Just Do It" attitude. In fact, the project soon became identified with that slogan. In the Spring of 1991, the Park and Recreation Department sought a downtown building or lot to use as an activity base. The search was unsuccessful because all of the on-market rental properties would have required substantial remodeling or investment to function as recreation centers, so the Park and Recreation Director scheduled a meeting with the Metro YMCA Executive Director. After a very short discussion about the need for evening programs to serve teens in the downtown area, both parties agreed that it needed to be done. In fact, the YMCA staff had discussed such a program for the past few years but no formal action was taken. The two Directors agreed to begin the program within two weeks at the Riverfront YMCA. Both agencies agreed to provide resources and solicit the support of other agencies. An exacerbating feeling of urgency existed, in large part, from recent trouble associated with the downtown loop-scooping activity.

Both Department and YMCA staff agreed that excessive up-front planning could kill the idea before it got off the ground. Instead, they made the decision to try the idea and work out problems as they occurred. The program began ten days later with the attendance of more than 200 youths. An advisory committee was appointed, and the program evolved into a successful venture which serves hundreds of teens on Friday and Saturday nights.

Normal Friday hours run from 9 p.m. to midnight and Saturday hours run from 7 p.m. to midnight. Special hours are sometimes scheduled. For example, in the spring after-prom alternatives run until 2 a.m. All participants are admitted free of charge. The program operates under a safe haven concept and promotes a "zero tolerance for violence" policy. The YMCA provides security, and the Des Moines Police Department provides an officer. Current programming is diverse and includes not only traditional sports activities but also a supervised free-weight room, music and dancing, field trips, and regularly scheduled movies. Spike Lee's *Malcolm X* was a recent feature attraction. Participants also run their own concession stand as a job-training project and program their own special events. Events scheduled during the summer of 1994 included a fashion show, a talent contest, and a battle of the bands. A Back to School—Stop the Violence dance was held in the fall of 1994. This successful event featured a live band, several speakers and attracted 1,400 participants. Funding was acquired to support a summer drama troupe which will stage their own productions including writing, set design, producing, performance, and travel. Ongoing funding for the drama troupe is still being sought. A modeling troupe evolved out of the fashion show. The troupe has done several other shows including an African Dress show for the City of Dubuque.

The program now sponsors a competitive basketball team which has hosted games and tournaments with both suburban and international (Italian) teams. Travel programs have also evolved. Six participants were selected to travel to Juarez, Mexico, in the summer of 1995. Finally, in response to the diverse needs of different age groups, seventeen- to nineteen-year-old participants are developing a weekly dance program separate from the activities most popular among younger participants.

VII. Marketing to Internal and/or External Publics

A local minority-operated radio station provided thousands of dollars in publicity to promote the program at no cost to the City or the YMCA. Also, they obtained significant news media coverage, due to the controversial nature of the project, both prior to the project's inception and following establishment of the program. Following development of the program, one of the reports filmed by the local ABC affiliate was picked up by other affiliates nationwide.

Program participants formed their own production company and have begun production of a television show focusing on teen issues. Funding was sought from several sources and has been provided by private corporate gifts and from a State of Iowa juvenile crime prevention grant. "Teen Talk" first aired in January 1995 on the TCI cable system under contract for 26 weekly shows. Negotiations are under way with the FOX network with respect to creating a long-term arrangement. Teen Talk airs from 8:00 to 9:00 on Saturday nights, usually in a talk show format where ideas are discussed by participants with divergent view points. Initial topics have included teen violence, teen pregnancy, race relations, gang affiliation, and education versus degeneration.

The set for Teen Talk was developed in-house by program participants. In addition to producing the show, the cast has also produced a documentary on how Teen Talk was developed and, in 1995, began production of a second documentary in conjunction with the Young Lawyers Association. The working title of the documentary is "As You Turn 18." It will feature discussion on the legal rights and responsibilities that accompany adulthood and will be distributed to school districts and public libraries.

VIII. Impact of Change on the Agency

This project served as an example of how a new regime of Park and Recreation Department administration could problem solve through collaboration. This project greatly enhanced the reputation of the Des Moines Park and Recreation Department.

Further, the program led to at least three additional positive outcomes: interest and support by the Milton Eisenhower Foundation; great role models for the hundreds of youth involved in the program; and an improved Park and Recreation staff attitude towards collaboration with other agencies. The YMCA and the City began other joint projects. The two organizations recently signed a lease agreement whereby, following renovations, the YMCA will assume programming responsibility for one of the City's community centers. Nearly $3 million will be spent on renovation, $1.75 million raised by the YMCA and $1 million raised by the City. The facility reopened in the fall of 1994. Outdoor activities such as golf, basketball and volleyball, scheduled during the summer of 1994, raised awareness of the Center's reopening. In addition to traditional programming, the Center will house offices for the Police Athletic League, job services offices, and provide space for a private daycare service. The City will retain responsibility for grounds and building maintenance.

IX. Impact of Change on the Community

Impact of the change was threefold. First, though not formally measured to date, merchants and residents reported a perception of improved safety in downtown Des Moines. Other spin-off programs and projects were introduced to enhance neighborhood recreation opportunities. As noted earlier, the city recently leased an inner-city community center to the YMCA. This arrangement will result in $2.75 million in building improvements and a more diverse programming mix.

Finally, the involvement of the Milton Eisenhower Foundation will undoubtedly have the most significant long-term impact. Due to the network built through this project, the Eisenhower Foundation is proposing to include Des Moines in its international community policing project. Des Moines city leaders traveled to Puerto Rico, France, and Japan to study how community policing collaborating with recreation improved neighborhoods.

X. Measurement of the Outcome

Originally, the expected results were measured in number of participants. To date the program continues to attract 250 to 350 participants every weekend. Local businesses have reported a dramatic drop in loop-scooping activity that continues to decrease. Des Moines police also report that the number of youth on the City's downtown streets dropped dramatically during weekend evening hours. Since this project resulted in many other collaborative projects, the scope of effect broadened not only in Des Moines, but throughout the state; departments in Cedar Rapids and Davenport are exploring similar cooperative arrangements. The results of community collaboration and enhanced neighborhood recreational service exceeded anticipated results.

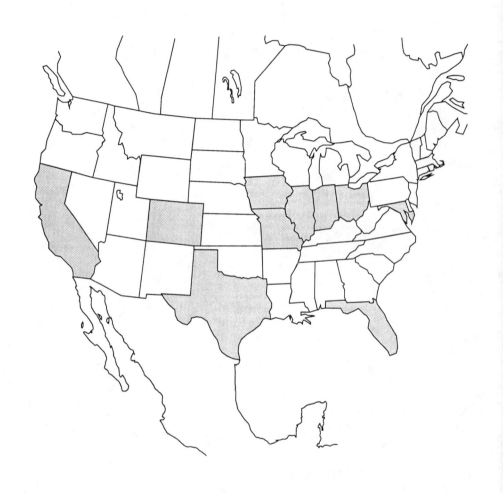

Concluding Comments

The projects described in this text are noteworthy for several reasons. As evident in the title, innovation is a common theme. Rogers (1983) noted that an innovation is an idea, practice, or object that is perceived as new. Whereas some projects discussed herein represent new variations on established themes, others are so innovative that governmental regulatory agencies are still struggling to classify them. The agencies and individuals highlighted within the book also exhibit clear bases for action. Although several of the projects took years in the making, the majority were remarkably quick to move from concept to implementation. A third common theme is the emphasis placed on service to community over service to agency. Although these two emphases are not necessarily incompatible, this book is replete with examples where agencies and the professionals comprising them willingly sacrificed the status quo and ventured into uncharted territory in search of workable paradigms for the 1990s and beyond. These models of change should prove helpful to motivate and facilitate change initiatives among parks and recreation professionals in other settings and communities.

Nevertheless, considerable work remains to be done. The emphasis of this book has, appropriately, been on describing the processes leading to change. Some of the change models are supported by extensive and impressive background research. The Anaheim, Austin and two Indiana Sports Corporation cases are the four which readily come to mind. Unfortunately, there is no guarantee that any of the resulting programs will be successful ultimately. Although the agencies and programs described in this book are universally committed to improving services and opportunities for their constituents, measurement of outcomes such as participant satisfaction and social progress remain problematic and often weak. Several exceptions are obvious, such as the excellent in-depth analysis referenced at the end of the two chapters related to Indiana Sports Corporation. However, research challenges are not so much unique to the cases described in this book as they are a reflection of the realities of the recreation profession. Evaluation procedures are too often considered in vague terms. Success is still too often monitored and expressed in terms of numbers through the door rather than by outcomes such as satisfaction. Numbers through the door are inadequate, though relatively easy to collect, and often a politically appealing substitute.

Certainly there are few tangible short-term rewards for recreation professionals seeking to document program effectiveness. Only recently, leisure and recreation professionals began to effectively quantify the benefits of recreation programming on a broad scale (e.g., Driver, Brown, & Peterson, 1991; Godbey, Graefe, & James, 1993). Why has this been the case? There are probably many explanations. Most professionals probably have more interest in providing services and getting things done than in measuring outcomes. That interest in service is likely why many chose the profession in the first place. As was noted earlier, professional reward systems, daily crises and operating pressures also inhibit research efforts regarding existing programs. In addition, many professionals lack research training. Research methods and statistics courses were proved rare in undergraduate level recreation and parks curricula even as late as ten to fifteen years ago. Today's undergraduate recreation and leisure studies majors, though not trained to be research scientists, usually have at least moderate levels of exposure to these concepts and they are aided in interpreting data by advances in accessible computer technology.

Several years ago Rabel Burdge (1985) wrote a provocative piece titled "The coming separation of leisure studies from parks and recreation education." Although Burdge was reflecting larger issues facing academics and practitioners within the field, the research dilemma outlined above represents a component of that conundrum. While Burdge's prophesy has not been fulfilled to date (indeed his essay produced immediate counterresponses from several authors including Godbey, 1985; Goodale, 1985; and Smith, 1985), the research-application dilemma and debate continues relatively unabated (e.g., Henderson, 1993; Nogradi, 1992). In addition to showcasing innovative program ideas, the Models of Change Conference framework may provide opportunities for bridging the research-practice gap. For example, leisure researchers have been developing and refining instrumentation related to leisure satisfaction, leisure boredom, leisure motivation, leisure involvement, self-esteem, serious leisure, and psychological commitment. But little of this research received widespread application among municipal recreation agencies. The nature of the programs and markets described in this book also suggest that qualitative research methodologies may be appropriate methods of inquiry in many cases. Few agencies have personnel who are trained to design and carry-out rigorous qualitative research.

Given the success of the first Models of Change Conference and the efforts to organize subsequent conferences, it may be possible to organize a short session each year devoted to documenting and solving problems related to the measurement of outcomes using cases from previous year's conferences. The conference may provide an effective forum for encouraging cooperative research efforts between academics and change-oriented agencies and professionals. It would probably work best if interested academics and interested professionals could be paired up to tackle issues specific to particular change models. Such university-agency cooperative efforts may provide opportunity for theory testing and rigorous measurement in heretofore unexplored ways. This idea represents a long-shot with respect to its ever becoming reality, but the same could be said for the original Models of Change Conference given the day-to-day demands facing most recreation professionals.

Good ideas tend to be found in clusters, advocated by innovative and fired-up people operating in agency cultures that facilitate and encourage change. Although the first Models of Change Conference overrepresented professionals and agencies from the Midwest, the capacity for innovation clearly exists for expanding the conference on a broader geographic scale. Future Models of Change Conferences will likely draw on professionals from a variety of regions. Models of Change may become an effective catalyst for diffusing positive change throughout the parks and recreation profession. Like the cases described in this book, the conference will likely be most effective if it continues to anticipate and adapt to changing circumstances.

Editor's References and Suggested Resources

Burdge, R. J. (1985). The coming separation of leisure studies from parks and recreation education. *Journal of Leisure Research, 17*, pp. 133-141.

Driver, B. L., Brown, P. J., and Peterson, G. L. (1991). *Benefits of leisure.* State College, PA: Venture Publishing, Inc.

Godbey, G. (1985). The coming cross-pollination of leisure studies and recreation and park education: A response. *Journal of Leisure Research, 17*, pp. 142-148.

Godbey, G., Graefe, A., and James, S. (1993). Reality and perception: Where do we fit in? *Parks and Recreation, 28*(1), pp. 76-83, 110-111.

Goodale, T. L. (1985). Carts before heavy mules: Are competing hypotheses too late? *Journal of Leisure Research, 17*, pp. 149-154.

Henderson, K. A. (1993). "The changer and the changed:" Leisure research in the 1990s. *Journal of Applied Recreation Research, 18*, pp. 1-16.

Henderson, K. A. and O'Neill, J. (1995). Has research contributed to the advancement of professional practice? *Parks and Recreation, 30*(1), pp. 17-20.

Nogradi, G. S. (1992). The potential for cooperation between academics and recreation practitioners: More a reality than a myth. *Journal of Applied Recreation Research, 17*, pp. 87-108.

Rogers, E. M. (1983). *Diffusion of innovations (3rd ed.).* New York, NY: The Free Press.

Smith, S. L. J. (1985). An alternative perspective on the nature of recreation and leisure studies: A personal response to Rabel Burdge. *Journal of Leisure Research, 17*, pp. 155-160.

Appendix A[8]

Cost Comparison of Mowing and Litter Collection

In House

Labor	+	*Equipment*	+	*Materials*
$20.50 mowing		$3.07 hourly costs		$1.20 gasoline, oil, and
23.00 litter control		0.48 repair costs		trash bags
0.12 clerical support		0.12 depreciation		0.32 uniforms, other
$43.62		$3.67		$1.52

Total In House Cost: $48.81 per acre

Contract

Direct Payment	+	*Labor*	+	*Materials*	+	*Advertisement*
$19.00		$1.38 inspection		$1.92 gas, oil		$0.11
		0.58 clerical support				
$19.00		$1.96		$1.92		$0.11

Total Contracted Cost: $22.99 per acre

Cost difference (Contract vs. In House): $25.82 per acre

Total savings per year—
1,600 (# contracted acres) x 14 (mowings per year) x $25.82 (cost difference) =
$578,368

---

[8] Companion information for "Successful and Effective Contracting of Maintenance Services," Kansas City, Missouri

Grounds Maintenance Service Specifications

Scope of Work:

Work shall consist of specified grounds maintenance activities upon specified Parks, Recreation and Boulevards properties within each defined area as scheduled.

Definitions:

a. **Grounds Maintenance Project Area** shall refer to specific geographic area(s) of the City designated to receive specified grounds maintenance services. See Section 2-E.

b. **Maintenance Schedule** shall mean the time periods established for the project year within which all prescribed maintenance activities for each area shall be completed.

c. **Maintenance Cycle** shall refer to each time period in the mowing schedule for the project year. Each time period is defined by a beginning and ending date, in which all prescribed maintenance activities for each area shall be completed.

d. **Area Inspector** shall mean the duly authorized representative of the Director of Parks, Recreation and Boulevards who shall monitor the contractors' progress within the Grounds Maintenance project area he/she is assigned to.

e. **Inclement Weather** shall mean rainy weather or when the condition of the soil is such that the rutting of property will not allow cutting of grass to be accomplished satisfactorily.

f. **Production Rate** shall refer to the amount of acres to be maintained per day based upon the total number of acres identified as remaining to be maintained in the mowing cycle.

   The production rate shall be calculated in the following manner:

$$\frac{\text{Total Acres Identified to be Maintained}}{\text{No. of Days Remaining in the Mowing Cycle}}$$

   For purposes of this contract, the minimum production rate shall be 25 acres per day.

g. **Trash and Litter** shall mean *any debris* within the Grounds Maintenance project area such as paper, cans, bottles, limbs three (3) inches or smaller in diameter, rocks, etc., which is not intended to be present as part of the landscape. Inclusive of entire project area including streets, side walks, curbs, hillsides, ditches, etc.... *Removal of debris will require sweeping of hard surface areas such as side walks and driveways.*

h. **Litter Removal** cycle shall mean the removal of trash and litter from the assigned Grounds Maintenance Project area as determined by the area inspector. The issuance of a work order for Litter Removal only, does not require mowing, trimming, edging, etc.

i. **Trimming** shall refer to the cutting or removal of all plant material immediately adjacent to or under park structures, trees, poles, tables, signs, fences, shrub beds, etc. Also includes removal of all plant material from expansion joints and any other cracks in curbs, side walks (both sides), driveways and any other concrete surface within the right of way.

j. **Edging** shall refer to the vertical removal of any and all plant material which encroaches over or onto side walks (both sides), curbs, steps, driveways and pavements. Edges shall be vertical, minimum depth of one (1) inch, and minimum width of one-quarter (1/4) inch.

k. **Chemical Trimming** shall refer to the use of a herbicide (such as Round Up and/or an approved equal containing a preemergent such as Surflan or an approved equal) as an alternative to the physical removal or cutting of plant material from areas to be trimmed. Approval for the application of herbicides must be obtained from the Area Inspector prior to herbicide application. Application must be in compliance with the Missouri Pesticide Use Act.

l. **Scalping** shall refer to any action which results in the mowing of any turf area below a three and one half (3-1/2) inch height down to and including the soil.

m. **Shrub Beds** shall mean any purposefully planted domestic, ornamental plant growth.

n. **Foreign Growth** shall include all weeds, thickets and noxious plants as defined in Chapter 18, Article VIII, Section 18.170, Code of General Ordinances.

o. **Mulch or Tree Rings** shall refer to those areas adjacent to trees, shrub beds, and other purposefully planted landscape areas in which all plant growth is removed.

p. **Sucker Growth** shall mean the incidental, vegetative growth arising from the bases and lower trunk areas of trees which are not essential to the overall well being of the plant.

Project Time Line

January
- Formal process of receiving bids and award of contracts based on lowest and best bid basis.

February
- Process contract documents.

March
- Meet with contractors individually.

April
- Initiate preseason service (e.g., edging).
- Issue notice to proceed.
- Complete contract approval process.

May
- Begin full-service operations on a routine cycle.
- Perform comprehensive inspections.

June
- Continue inspections, evaluations and counseling as necessary.
- Begin making a record of possible changes for next contract(s).
- Same as prior month.

July
- Same as prior month.
- Establish contract schedule for next season.

August
- Same as prior month.

September
- Prepare budget for next contract season.
- Same as prior month.

October
- Finalize draft of contract documents and specifications for next contract season.
- Begin closure of current contracts.
- Establish fall and winter schedules for services, if applicable.

November
- Have draft of contract documents approved.
- Advertise for next season's contractual service.
- Print contract documents and specifications.
- As current season contracts expire, process final payments and return performance bonds.

December
- Conduct prebid conference for next season's contracts.
- Meet with potential contractors for next season to inspect service areas.

Mowing and Minimal Litter Control

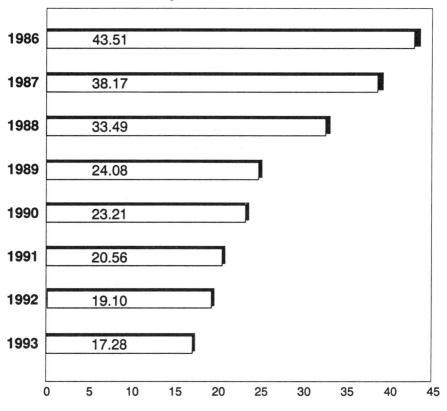

Mowing and minimal litter control

Year	Value
1986	43.51
1987	38.17
1988	33.49
1989	24.08
1990	23.21
1991	20.56
1992	19.10
1993	17.28

Dollar cost per acre ($)

Appendix B[9]

Golf Course Proposal Evaluation Sheet: Weighted Price and Nonprice Attributes

Contract No. _____ Name of Contract Proposer: _____
Date: _____

Attributes	Grading 0 - 4 Team Score	Weight	Price Index
Relevant Experience			
Track Record			
Technical Skills			
Resources			
Management Skills			
Methodology			
Quality of the Proposal			
	Sum of Nonprice Attributes (A):		

Price Guide
Price Index = Grade x Weight = _____(B)
Overall Index = (A) + (B) =

Evaluation Team

Team Leader _____ Evaluator _____

Evaluator _____ Evaluator _____

Evaluator _____ Evaluator _____

Evaluator _____ Evaluator _____

---

[9] Companion information for "Private Management of Public Golf Courses," Indianapolis, Indiana.

The A•B•Cs of Behavior Change: Skills for Working with Behavior Problems in Nursing Homes
        by Margaret D. Cohn, Michael A. Smyer and Ann L. Horgas
Activity Experiences and Programming Within Long-Term Care
        by Ted Tedrick and Elaine R. Green
The Activity Gourmet
        by Peggy Powers
Advanced Concepts for Geriatric Nursing Assistants
        by Carolyn A. McDonald
Adventure Education
        edited by John C. Miles and Simon Priest
Assessment: The Cornerstone of Activity Programs
        by Ruth Perschbacher
*At-Risk Youth and Gangs—A Resource Manual for the Parks and Recreation Professional—
        Expanded and Updated*
        by The California Park and Recreation Society
Benefits of Leisure
        edited by B. L. Driver, Perry J. Brown and George L. Peterson
Benefits of Recreation Research Update
        by Judy M. Sefton and W. Kerry Mummery
Beyond Bingo: Innovative Programs for the New Senior
        by Sal Arrigo, Jr., Ann Lewis and Hank Mattimore
The Community Tourism Industry Imperative—The Necessity, The Opportunities, Its Potential
        by Uel Blank
Dimensions of Choice: A Qualitative Approach to Recreation, Parks, and Leisure Research
        by Karla A. Henderson
Evaluating Leisure Services: Making Enlightened Decisions
        by Karla A. Henderson with M. Deborah Bialeschki
Evaluation of Therapeutic Recreation Through Quality Assurance
        edited by Bob Riley
The Evolution of Leisure: Historical and Philosophical Perspectives
        by Thomas Goodale and Geoffrey Godbey
The Game Finder—A Leader's Guide to Great Activities
        by Annette C. Moore
Great Special Events and Activities
        by Annie Morton, Angie Prosser and Sue Spangler
Inclusive Leisure Services: Responding to the Rights of People with Disabilities
        by John Dattilo
Internships in Recreation and Leisure Services: A Practical Guide for Students
        by Edward E. Seagle, Jr., Ralph W. Smith and Lola M. Dalton
Interpretation of Cultural and Natural Resources
        by Douglas M. Knudson, Ted T. Cable and Larry Beck
Introduction to Leisure Services—7th Edition
        by H. Douglas Sessoms and Karla A. Henderson
Leadership and Administration of Outdoor Pursuits, Second Edition
        by Phyllis Ford and James Blanchard
Leisure And Family Fun (LAFF)
        by Mary Atteberry-Rogers
The Leisure Diagnostic Battery: Users Manual and Sample Forms
        by Peter A. Witt and Gary Ellis

Δ Other Books By Venture Publishing

Leisure Diagnostic Battery Computer Software
 by Gary Ellis and Peter A. Witt
Leisure Education: A Manual of Activities and Resources
 by Norma J. Stumbo and Steven R. Thompson
Leisure Education II: More Activities and Resources
 by Norma J. Stumbo
Leisure Education: Program Materials for Persons with Developmental Disabilities
 by Kenneth F. Joswiak
Leisure Education Program Planning: A Systematic Approach
 by John Dattilo and William D. Murphy
Leisure in Your Life: An Exploration, Fourth Edition
 by Geoffrey Godbey
A Leisure of One's Own: A Feminist Perspective on Women's Leisure
 by Karla Henderson, M. Deborah Bialeschki, Susan M. Shaw and
  Valeria J. Freysinger
Leisure Services in Canada: An Introduction
 by Mark S. Searle and Russell E. Brayley
Leveraging the Benefits of Parks and Recreation: The Phoenix Project
 by The California Park and Recreation Society
Marketing for Parks, Recreation, and Leisure
 by Ellen L. O'Sullivan
Outdoor Recreation Management: Theory and Application, Third Edition
 by Alan Jubenville and Ben Twight
Planning Parks for People
 by John Hultsman, Richard L. Cottrell and Wendy Zales Hultsman
Private and Commercial Recreation
 edited by Arlin Epperson
The Process of Recreation Programming Theory and Technique, Third Edition
 by Patricia Farrell and Herberta M. Lundegren
Protocols for Recreation Therapy Programs
 edited by Jill Kelland, along with the Recreation Therapy Staff at Alberta
  Hospital Edmonton
Quality Management: Applications for Therapeutic Recreation
 edited by Bob Riley
Recreation and Leisure: Issues in an Era of Change, Third Edition
 edited by Thomas Goodale and Peter A. Witt
*The Recreation Connection to Self-Esteem—A Resource Manual for the Park, Recreation and
  Community Services Professional*
 by The California Park and Recreation Society
Recreation Economic Decisions: Comparing Benefits and Costs
 by Richard G. Walsh
Recreation Programming and Activities for Older Adults
 by Jerold E. Elliott and Judith A. Sorg-Elliott
Reference Manual for Writing Rehabilitation Therapy Treatment Plans
 by Penny Hogberg and Mary Johnson
Research in Therapeutic Recreation: Concepts and Methods
 edited by Marjorie J. Malkin and Christine Z. Howe
Risk Management in Therapeutic Recreation: A Component of Quality Assurance
 by Judith Voelkl

A Social History of Leisure Since 1600
        by Gary Cross
The Sociology of Leisure
        by John R. Kelly and Geoffrey Godbey
A Study Guide for National Certification in Therapeutic Recreation
        by Gerald O'Morrow and Ron Reynolds
Therapeutic Recreation: Cases and Exercises
        by Barbara C. Wilhite and M. Jean Keller
Therapeutic Recreation in the Nursing Home
        by Linda Buettner and Shelley L. Martin
Therapeutic Recreation Protocol for Treatment of Substance Addictions
        by Rozanne W. Faulkner
*A Training Manual for Americans With Disabilities Act Compliance in Parks and Recreation
    Settings*
        by Carol Stensrud
Understanding Leisure and Recreation: Mapping the Past, Charting the Future
        edited by Edgar L. Jackson and Thomas L. Burton

  Venture Publishing, Inc.
1999 Cato Avenue
State College, PA 16801
Phone: (814) 234-4561; FAX: (814) 234-1651